Annette Sills

Derailed

POOLBEG

This book is a work of fiction. The names, characters, places, businesses, organisations and incidents portrayed in it are either the product of the author's imagination or are used fictitiously. Any resemblance to actual persons, living or dead, events or locales is entirely coincidental.

Published 2024 by Poolbeg Press Ltd.

123 Grange Hill, Baldoyle, Dublin 13, Ireland

Email: poolbeg@poolbeg.com

© Annette Sills 2024

The moral right of the author has been asserted.

© Poolbeg Press Ltd. 2024, copyright for editing, typesetting, layout, design, ebook and cover image.

A catalogue record for this book is available from the British Library.

ISBN 978178199-535-8

All rights reserved. No part of this publication may be reproduced or transmitted in any form or by any means, electronic or mechanical, including photography, recording, or any information storage or retrieval system, without permission in writing from the publisher. The book is sold subject to the condition that it shall not, by way of trade or otherwise, be lent, resold or otherwise circulated without the publisher's prior consent in any form of binding or cover other than that in which it is published and without a similar condition, including this condition, being imposed on the subsequent purchaser.

www.poolbeg.com

About the Author

Annette Sills was born in Wigan, Lancashire, to parents from County Mayo, Ireland. Her short stories have been longlisted and shortlisted in a number of competitions including the Fish Short Story Prize, *Books Ireland Magazine* and the *Telegraph* Short Story Club. Her first novel, *The Relative Harmony of Julie O'Hagan*, was shortlisted in Rethink Press New Novels Competition 2014. Her novel, *My Mother's Children*, was published by Poolbeg Press.

Annette writes historical and contemporary stories set in the Manchester Irish Diaspora. She is fascinated by migration and belonging, mental health and the dynamics of family life.

She currently lives in Chorlton, Manchester, with her husband and two children.

Acknowledgements

Heartfelt thanks to:

Emily Hughes, Bernadette Curran, Jimmy Curran, Ginny McKay, Claire Winstanley, Jenny Raddings, David Llewelyn and Anita McSorley for your invaluable input. Cheers, Jessica French, for the title.

The wonderful team at Poolbeg, Paula Campbell, and my keen-eyed editor Gaye Shortland.

My Short Story Club pals, thank you for your help and laughter, especially in difficult times.

My extended Irish family, your shenanigans have been a source of joy to me over the years.

Nick, for his continuing love and support in my writing endeavours, and Jimmy and Ciara xx

Dedication

This book is dedicated to my wonderful children Jimmy and Ciara, and their peers xx

PART ONE

CHAPTER 1

Manchester

May 2016

Eileen

Was there anyone quite like Michelle McGreevy for being late? Eileen stared down at the raindrops dancing on the scuffed toes of her boots. If Michelle didn't show up in five minutes, she was leaving.

Just as she was about to give up hope, she spotted Michelle's copper head of curls by the entrance to the woods, and she puddle-dodged across the car park to join her.

"In all the sixteen years I've known you, I don't think you've ever been on time for anything," Eileen remarked as they headed down the path by the side of the swollen brook. Murky water tumbled over rocks, swirling up sediment and carrying fallen branches in its current.

"It's seventeen years, actually," Michelle replied.

Eileen tilted her head to one side. "You're right. We met when we were pregnant, didn't we?"

Michelle grimaced. "Those awful NCT classes. Birthing balls everywhere. Learning to breastfeed with those dolls with faces like Chuckie. *Urgh!*"

Eileen stopped walking, turned to face Michelle with her hands on her hips, and grinned. "I actually liked those classes."

"I know. You were such an Earth Mother back then. Anne and I hated them. Remember when the midwife handed Anne one of the dolls and she recoiled in horror and said, 'Darling, I can't possibly put my nipple near that'?"

Eileen threw her head back and laughed. "That's Anne for you! Always saying it as it is. We were so much older than the other mothers, weren't we?"

"I think the polite term was 'geriatric mother'. No doubt there's some new PC version now."

"And now Meg, Nathan, and Alex are about to leave Chorlton High. It feels like yesterday they were starting Broadoak Primary. Where did those years go?"

They trudged on, a sudden deluge forcing them to shelter under a clump of pine trees.

Eileen wiped a drop of rain from her nose. "A gang of lads followed Alex home from school yesterday," she said.

"You're kidding," Michelle said, tightening the hood of her Burberry jacket. "Is he OK?"

"He was a bit shaken up when it happened but he's grand now." Eileen dug the toe of her boot into the wet ground. "The little gobshites left us a charming little message on our garden wall."

"Really? I won't ask what. Nathan hasn't said anything about anyone going after him, but then he never tells me anything."

"Who the hell would go after Nathan? He's built like a small van, and he's on friendly terms with all the gangsters in year eleven."

Michelle nodded and sighed. "True."

An awkward silence hung in the air and the rain hammered down around them.

"The school won't exclude our boys, will they, Michelle?" Eileen asked tentatively.

"*Nah*. Not so close to their GCSE's."

"I feckin' hope not."

"You're worrying too much, pet. What they did was a stupid one-off. Boys that age make all kinds of monumentally daft decisions. The frontal cortex of the sixteen-year-old male brain is a nightmare. Trust me – I've learned that much as a doctor."

The rain stopped as abruptly as it had started. They walked over the iron bridge, and on in the direction of the river, mud squelching under their feet. Known locally as The Meadows, Chorlton Ees was a vast nature reserve that hugged the River Mersey. Considering its city location, it was surprisingly rich in flora, fauna, and wildlife. On recent walks, they had spotted a kingfisher, a water vole, and only last week a clutch of parakeets on a telegraph pole. They'd stood for ages and marvelled at the exotic dots of green and yellow against the leaden Manchester sky. Even on a grim day in May like this, Eileen loved being down here, cocooned in the woods, away from the smells and sounds of the city. It reminded her of home, the soggy little village back in County Mayo she'd left some years before.

When the Head of Chorlton High had called to tell her about the photo that was circulating around the school, Eileen was convinced they had the wrong Alex. She was in denial right up until the moment at the meeting when she saw the picture with her own eyes. Her heart had fallen with the speed of a falling lift. She was a teacher herself. She taught ESOL in a Further Education college, not a High School, but she could imagine the mayhem a photo like that could create. How could Alex, her gentle, tree-hugger of a boy, be involved in something like that? She was still trying to get her head around it.

They ploughed on to the river. The olive-green water surged forward relentlessly, spilling out onto its muddy banks, and pylons and high rises dotted the landscape everywhere. Closing her eyes, she pictured the lake back home. It was turquoise and silver on summer days and, in winter, the morning mist peeled away to reveal the swell of the Twelve Bens mountains in the distance, Connemara's finest.

She felt Michelle's hand tapping her shoulder. "Sorry, I was miles away."

"You blame Nathan for what happened, don't you?"

"I do not."

"You think he's turning out like his dad."

"That's not true. Alex has to take responsibility for what he did too. It was so out of character, though. He's such a softie."

"Whereas Nathan is a thug."

"I never said that."

Michelle looked glumly ahead, her large pale-blue eyes suddenly widening. "*Christ on a bike!*" she said, looking at her watch. "I knew there was something. I'm supposed to be at a meeting in the hospital in an hour."

"I thought it was your day off?"

"It is."

They ran back through the woods to Chorltonville, the upmarket area where Michelle lived. By the time they arrived at the end of her long gravel drive, they were both doubled over and panting.

Eileen held on to the stitch in her left hip. "Thanks for the surprise 5k."

Michelle gave her a thumbs-up. "Anytime."

Eileen watched her head up the drive and pick up Nathan's bike where he'd abandoned it in the bushes.

"*Tosser!*" Michelle yelled.

Eileen smiled. She could never be cross with Michelle for long. She loved her far too much for that.

Michelle

Michelle left the traffic behind in Chorlton High Street, put her foot down, and sped along Wilbraham Road. How the hell had the meeting slipped her mind? Probably because she had so much on her plate with Nathan recently. He was an ongoing project. She couldn't decide which was harder: parenting him or working a manic Saturday-night shift at the hospital. Both involved a lot of carnage and an abundance of tolerance and patience – qualities she was rapidly running out of.

It hurt to think Eileen blamed Nathan for what had happened at the school. She definitely did, despite her denials. Nathan and Alex had grown up together, for God's sake. For some reason Eileen seemed to think Nathan had dragged Alex kicking and screaming into the whole sorry affair. According to Nathan, it couldn't be further from the truth.

"Alex was mad to join in," he'd said, when she probed him. "He's Billy No-mates so I let him tag along."

"That's sad. You and Meg and Alex used to be so close."

He frowned. "Just because you and Anne and Eileen are bosom buddies doesn't mean Meg and Alex and me will be too. I've got my own mates now."

Michelle turned up the car radio. A woman from the Vote Leave Campaign was being interviewed about next month's referendum. She was saying that if Vote Leave got in, they would give the £350 million a week the country currently gave to the EU to the NHS instead.

"My arse you would!" she muttered, switching to Smooth FM.

Mylene Klass was playing Springsteen's "The River", a special request from husband Paul to wife Mary thanking her for thirty wonderful years of marriage. The Boss had been the soundtrack of her and her ex's early years together, and "The River" had always been one of her favourite songs. It told the story of two young lovers who have to get married – then their dreams for the future quickly fade due to the hard realities of life, ultimately leading to hopelessness. It was a sad song, not a celebratory one. Bad choice, Paul.

She stopped at the traffic lights in Fallowfield, her old uni stomping ground. Students with multi-coloured backpacks, clunky shoes, and pink-and-blue hair were milling around outside a plush new hall of residence. Blocks like this were springing up on every corner of the city. They had names like City Life and Artisan Heights, and had gyms, cinema rooms and libraries. She and Rob had met at the university. They'd lived in their fair share of grotty student house shares in Fallowfield. She once knew these streets like the veins on the back of her hand. Not anymore. Like so much of the city, the area was changing beyond recognition.

She drove on to the hospital through Rusholme and Wilmslow Road, an area known as Curry Mile. That was changing too. It was once home to over seventy of Manchester's best South Asian restaurants. The food was dirt cheap and out of the world, and at weekends people would queue around the block to get a table or a late-night takeaway. Only a few of the old haunts remained now. Many had been replaced by pawn shops, shisha bars, and Polish supermarkets.

As she neared the hospital, Michelle's thoughts returned to the meeting at the school. Rob had been such an arse. She could have throttled him.

When she'd arrived he'd been sitting in the ante-room near reception, dressed in pinstripes, a pink shirt, and his old school tie. He'd put on even more weight since she last saw him. His jacket was bursting at the seams and his belly flopped over the waistband of his trousers, like an extra limb. He was back from Marbella, where he'd taken early retirement with Jane, a peroxide blonde from Stockport, with a suspiciously smooth forehead and large collection of leopard-print leggings. The pair of them had been having an affair for five years before she'd found out.

She'd sat down at the far end of the long table.

"Why are you dressed like a defence lawyer?" she asked. "And what's with the old school tie? Do you think they won't expel your son because you went to a posh boarding school?"

Rob rolled his eyes. "Hello to you too, darling."

She looked him up and down. "Are you keeping an eye on your blood pressure?"

"Oh, here we go!"

"Seriously, Rob, you need to lay off the Rioja and the chorizo."

"Stop nagging. We're divorced, remember?"

She shrugged. "Hey, what do I know? I'm only a doctor."

Eileen and Sergio arrived shortly afterwards. Neither of them had seen Rob since the divorce and the four of them sat in an uneasy silence.

Rob cracked a lame joke about waiting outside the headmaster's office for the cane, and Sergio responded with a smile that didn't reach his eyes.

Eileen avoided all eye contact with Rob and scrolled on her phone. Her contempt for him was written in big fat letters all over her face.

Being in the same room again with Sergio, Eileen and Rob made Michelle feel nostalgic. She thought about the evenings the four of them used to spend together, along with Anne and Hakim, when the kids were little. Each family would take it in turns to host. Meg, Alex, and Nathan would run themselves ragged in the garden, then fall asleep in front of *Toy Story* or *The Cat in the Hat*, while the adults ate and drank and put the world to rights. They were good times. She experienced a sudden wrench of sadness. Her marriage hadn't survived, while the others had.

Michelle glanced around the room. One poster advertised a local LGBT support group, another announced auditions for an upcoming production of *West Side Story*, and the words *Tolerance, Respect*, and *Kindness* were inked on the wall above the whiteboard. Her mouth suddenly dry, she got herself a cup of water from the cooler in the corner.

Chorlton High was considered the best state secondary for miles around. A sprawling inner-city comp, it had eighteen hundred students from a broad demographic, and a high number of pupils with special educational needs, whilst maintaining consistently good exam results. It was also very hot on inclusion and diversity.

As Michelle sat back down, the Head, Sian Evans, entered the room. Sian was a Welsh no-nonsense type, who smiled a lot, and was highly regarded by parents and students alike. Plump and fresh-faced, that day she was wearing a baggy purple dress that made her look like a juicy grape.

She got straight to the point. Turning on her iPad, she showed them the photo that had been circulating around the school. It had been taken at a rally organised by the Vote Leave Campaign, and it showed Nathan and Alex in their school uniforms standing with some other boys whom Michelle did not know. Nathan was grinning and giving a thumbs-up, Alex cowering behind him. Above their heads were a number of Union Jacks and a large banner saying, "*Muslims out – Britain First – No More Mosques*".

Michelle swallowed. Nathan had really excelled himself this time. What in the name of Jesus had he been thinking?

Sian switched off the iPad and placed it on the table in front of her. "The photo has been circulating around the school, causing conflict and problems for teachers and students alike," she said. "I can't begin to tell you how many emails and phone calls we've received from parents. Chorlton High prides itself on being inclusive and tolerant. I'm afraid behaviour like this is not compatible with our values."

"Alex will never do anything like this again, I promise you," Sergio interjected nervously.

Eileen mumbled in assent and Michelle nodded. Rob folded his arms, rested them on top his paunch, and exhaled loudly.

Sian continued. "Hopefully, this incident is a one-off. However, I'm going to have to exclude both boys for a week."

Michelle sighed in relief. She'd expected far worse.

"Surely you can't exclude a child for something that didn't happen on school premises?" said Rob.

Sian threw him a withering look that Michelle suspected she kept for challenging year-eleven boys. "It's not quite as simple as that, Mr Grainger," she replied curtly.

Rob shook his head. "It was a Vote Leave rally, for God's sake, not a riot organised by the National Front! Whatever happened to freedom of speech?"

"The problem is the photograph. The boys are in school uniform and pictured in front of a banner supporting Britain First, a far-right, fascist party. The fact that the group may have hijacked the Vote Leave rally is irrelevant. The banner stating *Muslims Out* clearly suggests racial hatred." She fiddled with a paper file in front of her. "I'm afraid any further incidents could result in the boys being assessed under the government's counterterrorism strategy – Prevent." She pulled a number of leaflets out of the file and passed them around. "You can read all about Prevent here. It's an initiative to stop young people becoming involved in terrorism and joining extremist groups."

Rob snatched up a leaflet, his thick gold watch sliding down his cuff. "You have *got* to be joking!"

"We have to take these things seriously, Mr Grainger. Not that long ago, one of our staff members reported a student to the authorities, as he was suspected of attending a gathering of Islamic extremists. It came to nothing in the end, as it happens. The rally Alex and Nathan attended is no different."

Michelle put her reading glasses on and scanned the leaflet. It seemed a bit extreme to her, but she wasn't going to argue. She'd do anything to get Nathan through his last months of school and his GCSE's.

Rob was turning a dark shade of puce. "Alex and Nathan are not terrorists," he growled. "They're sixteen-year-old boys having a bit of a lark."

Sian sat back. "Nobody is calling them terrorists, but as a school we have to deal with this. I'm afraid if anything like this happens again both boys will be permanently excluded. And that includes exclusion from exam revision classes."

Rob stood up, his chair scraping like chalk on a blackboard. Everybody winced.

"For Christ's sake, stop being such a dick and sit down!" snapped Michelle.

"*You*," he said, jabbing a forefinger at her, "*you* need to stand up for our son."

He snatched his camel coat from a chair, where he'd laid it, carefully folded, then marched to the door. "Exclude them for a couple of days, if you must, but this is political correctness gone bonkers." Scrunching up the leaflet, he aimed it at the bin on his way out, missing by a mile.

Michelle lowered her eyes and mumbled apologies. Gathering her things, she made a quick exit and caught up with Rob in the school car park a few minutes later.

"*What the hell?*" she hissed. "I only invited you to the meeting because I wanted you to see what I put up with from Nathan on a daily basis while you're sitting on your arse by the pool drinking cocktails with Jane. He's your only child, for Christ's sake! You never even call me to ask how he's doing."

He folded his arms. "Not very well, by the look of things."

"If you must know, he's a proper little bastard these days." She suddenly felt her voice quiver. "I don't know what's got into him."

Rob's face softened. "I'll have a word with him. But there really isn't a lot I can do, Michelle. I live in Spain now."

As she watched him stride across the car park, tears ran down her cheeks. Two years had passed since he'd left her for Jane, but the rage and hurt and frustration she experienced whenever she saw him had never gone away.

Michelle arrived at the hospital with five minutes to spare before her meeting. As the revolving doors spat her into the packed reception area, her phone pinged in her pocket. It was a text from Tony from the dating app. They'd been chatting for a couple of weeks now, and he wanted to meet up at a bar in town, but could she really be arsed? She'd been on scores of dates since she'd signed up, but none of them had led to anything meaningful.

She elbowed her way through the crowd of waiting patients. "Fuck you for leaving me, Rob Grainger," she muttered under her breath.

Then she quickly texted Tony back, suggesting a bar in the Northern Quarter.

Anne

Anne gathered the dirty dinner plates and glanced over at Eileen and Michelle. They were standing at her kitchen island, sozzled, and slicing the lemon drizzle cake she'd baked for Eileen's birthday.

Not for the first time, it struck Anne how different her best friends were in every way. Michelle had a bovine figure, with wide hips and short sturdy legs. She resembled one of those Irish dolls Anne had seen in a shop at Dublin airport once: copper corkscrew, large pale-blue eyes, and pronounced freckles. Michelle was always on the go. A pragmatist, she possessed a northern bluntness that Anne, a Londoner, found mostly hilarious, but at times disarming.

While everything about Michelle was round and curvy, Eileen was all length and angles. Enviably tall at five feet ten, she had an athletic figure, with broad shoulders, long fingers, and feet the size of small canoes. Her strong jaw and sturdy features rendered her more handsome than beautiful, and her blue-black hair and brown eyes gave her a Mediterranean rather than an Irish look. She had that lovely Irish lilt, though. Softly spoken and laid-back, her mouth always looked like it was teetering on a smile. Eileen was one of the most chilled people she knew, and a great diplomat when it came to friendship. Recently, she had added a streak of blonde to her French bob. It looked quirky, not cheap. Anne was rather envious. She could never get away with anything as daring as that.

Eileen and Michelle were Irish. Eileen was the real deal and Michelle had been born in Manchester to a fervent republican family from Belfast. They were very close, and Anne felt like a third leg in the friendship at times. She didn't mind, though. Together, her friends created an atmosphere of high spirits and joie de vivre. Being around them felt like sitting in a hot tub of bubbles. They'd been having such a hoot tonight. She couldn't remember the last time she'd heard so much laughter in the house.

The three of them sat at the table with a bottle of port, and the cake. They toasted Eileen.

"Darlings, I feel terribly guilty for saying this," said Anne, putting her glass down, "but I felt a wave of relief when Meg and Hakim left this morning."

"Where are they?" asked Michelle.

"At Aisha's in Altringham. Hakim finally persuaded Meg to go for a few days. Aisha is her favourite stepsister and she adores her little nephew Zaidan. The plan is to get her involved in his birthday party tomorrow to distract her from her studies for a while." Anne sipped her port. "She hasn't left her room in weeks. I can't believe I've got two whole days to myself. No treading on eggshells, no meltdowns, no keeping an eye on everything she does or doesn't eat, no waking up in the early hours to the sound of her pacing her room, or finding her hunched over her desk, bug-eyed and crying because she can't understand the notes that her chemistry teacher has sent home."

Eileen squeezed her arm. "I had no idea things were that bad."

"It's been hell, Eileen. It's now six months since she stopped going to school and we've been cooped up together twenty-four seven. The homeschooling and constant meltdowns are totally exhausting. I can't tell you how grateful I am for this one evening of respite."

Yet, despite her need to switch off from it all, she been texting Hakim all day for updates on how Meg was doing and she'd limited herself to a couple of glasses of booze in case she had to drive over to Altrincham in an emergency.

Hakim had replied about an hour ago. "**Meg's absolutely fine. But I'm starting to wonder which one of you has anxiety issues.**"

Despite the smiling emojis, she knew he was getting shirty, so she hadn't texted since.

The three of them were tucking into the cake when Michelle's phone rang. Rolling her eyes, she left the room to take a call from Nathan.

Eileen put her plate to one side and sat back. "I can't eat any more. I'm so full after Hakim's delicious curry. That dahl was outstanding."

"He got up early this morning to make it," Anne said.

"You're so lucky to be married to such a fantastic cook."

"I know."

Hakim's samosas were the reason they met. They were both working at the same Further Education College – she was teaching art and he was working in the IT department. One day she was sitting opposite him in the canteen and she commented on how yummy his lunch looked. He told her the samosas were home-made and insisted she try one. Then they struck up a conversation about food. He told her he'd never cooked in his life until he'd been suddenly widowed and left with three hungry teenage daughters to feed. From that day on they sat together every lunchtime. She quickly fell for his Omar Sharif looks and self-deprecating wit, but he was dreadfully slow on the uptake. She was the one who ended up asking him out.

A year later she moved into Brantingham Road, pregnant with Meg at the ripe old age of forty-two. Nadia and Aisha had left for university by then, and Farah left the following year. When she developed a sweet tooth later in her pregnancy, Hakim took up baking: macaroons, Victoria Sponge, tiramisu, chocolate brownies. You name it, he baked it. She and Meg had tried to get him to go on *The Great British Bake Off*, but he said he was camera shy and having none of it.

"So, tell me about Meg. Is she getting much support from the school these days?"

"They send work home and mark it, but that's about it."

"What about one-to-one tutoring?"

"God, no. Nobody gets that. There are so many kids at that school with mental-health issues. There simply aren't the resources. Many haven't got the support at home that Meg has, either. She's never going to be a priority for them so close to the exams."

"Poor love. Will she make it in for her exams?"

"God knows. At least we've got a CAMHS appointment now." Eileen looked blank.

"CAMHS is the Children and Adolescent Mental Health Services. It's been six months since the school made a referral."

"Six months? Are you serious?"

"Getting help has been a total nightmare. Meg stopped seeing the private counsellor we got her. The woman hadn't a clue how to deal with young people and Meg hated her. The best help is with CAMHS, but the waiting lists are months long."

"Christ."

"It's an epidemic, Eileen. At our last school meeting, the attendance officer told me school refusal has always been an issue, but in recent years she was seeing a huge increase in middle-class girls like Meg dropping like flies in years ten and eleven. The numbers for self-harming, eating disorders and anxiety disorders are going through the roof."

"God, it's everywhere, isn't it?"

Michelle returned, mumbling something about Nathan having lost his bus pass and wanting money for a cab. As she sat back down at the table, she picked up one of the sculptures from the shelving unit behind her chair. A cowed head with two hands covering a face, painted in bronze, it was one of the last things Anne had made before she had to stop work at Clay Corner, the pottery studio she owned, to stay at home with Meg.

"I love this." Michelle turned the sculpture over in her hands. "I was passing Clay Corner the other day. I saw the new girl. She was with a big group of kids painting mugs. It looked busy."

"I wish." Anne sighed. "Sophie's dreadful. She's terribly disorganised and she keeps giving customers the wrong pots to take home. She can't add up properly either, but I can't afford to pay anyone better. The rent's just gone up too. If I don't get back in there myself soon, I might have to close."

"You're kidding?" Michelle put the sculpture back.

"I can't see any other way. Someone's got to stay home with Meg and get her through her GCSE's. Hakim can't. He's the main wage earner."

Michelle dug her fork into her cake. "Can't you bribe her to go to school?"

"It's not as simple as that. Meg isn't refusing school out of wilfulness. She's experiencing high levels of anxiety and having panic attacks. She isn't well enough to go in."

"How about taking her phone off her?"

Eileen threw Michelle a warning glance.

"You simply don't get it, do you, Michelle?" snapped Anne. "I can no more bribe Meg to go into school every day than you can bribe a patient with a broken leg to climb Mount Everest!"

Feeling herself suddenly welling up, Anne got up from the table, went over to the sink and poured herself a glass of water. She looked out of the window, her eyes drawn to the dramatic sky. The day had been fine, but now grey-and-black clouds were gathering, like an army, and swallowing up the remaining pink slithers of evening light.

She turned around at the touch of Michelle's hand on her shoulder.

"Sorry, pet." Michelle enfolded her in a bear hug. "I'm a bit pissed. Take no notice of me."

Anne drove them both home later. In the car, Eileen told Michelle she'd seen an old video clip of her granny on YouTube. Apparently, Michelle's relative was a leading figure in the Women for Peace organisation during the years of conflict in Northern Ireland.

"She looked mighty – the way she was giving out to all those men in suits outside Stormont in that treacly Belfast accent," said Eileen.

"Oh yes, Granny McGreevy was some woman," replied Michelle.

Anne stiffened and stared at the road ahead. She loved Michelle and Eileen dearly but she hated it when they talked about "The Troubles" and went into Irish rebel mode: the songs, the flag-waving, the rants about Irish history and politics. The volume was always turned up when they'd had a few drinks. Words like *Paras* and *RUC* and *Provos* would fire around her like arrows. It made her close up like a clam.

After she dropped Michelle in Chorltonville, she took Eileen on to the estate where she lived. She and Sergio had bought an ex-council house there for next to nothing long before Chorlton became *the* trendy place to live in Manchester and the house prices rocketed.

She was still smarting after the earlier conversation with Michelle about Meg's school refusal. She'd never had Michelle down as an Unbeliever. She'd met quite a few since Meg first became unwell: other parents, so-called friends, teachers who didn't believe that poor mental health in children was even a thing. People who should know better. She could spot an Unbeliever a mile off. Their kids had no issues at all and, the minute she mentioned Meg's problems, they'd narrow their eyes and give her a sceptical look that said, "*Your daughter isn't ill. She's refusing to go to school because of your sloppy parenting. You mollycoddled her in her early years, and now she has no resilience. You've turned her into a snowflake.*"

Anne pulled up outside Eileen's house, her gaze landing on a whitewashed slash of paint along the garden wall.

"Don't ask," said Eileen glumly as she got out of the car.

Anne was about to drive off when she heard the low thrum of rap coming from the house opposite where a huge St. George's flag fluttered at an upstairs window. Her eyes rested on two girls sitting on the doorstep. They were about Megan's age, dressed in identical miniscule skirts, with hooped earrings and their hair scraped back in buns. They were huddled around a phone, laughing. Anne pulled away, feeling an ache of sadness. Meg should be hanging out with friends like that on a Saturday night, not held prisoner in her room by anxiety and fear.

As she drove home, the pregnant clouds she'd noticed earlier finally burst and the rain came down in torrents.

CHAPTER 2

Eileen

Sergio was about to put his key in the front door when she put her hand on his shoulder to stop him. They'd just arrived home after an evening at the San Juan tapas bar on Beech Road to celebrate her birthday, and they were both tiddly. She could hear music coming from inside the living room. Forefinger on her lip, she tiptoed to the window and peered through a chink in the curtain. In the honey-coloured lamp light, she could see Alex dancing around the room to "Love My Way" by the Psychedelic Furs. His eyes were shut tight, and he was singing with an intense expression on his face. She'd never seen him dance before and he was good. His long limbs moved fluidly to the beat, and he had a swivel in his hips. He looked beautiful. Transfixed, she watched for longer than she should have. The song reminded her of her cousin Shannon back home. They'd been more like sisters than cousins growing up. When they were fifteen, Shannon had played her "Love My Way", and said, "I'm gay and this is my anthem".

Both she and Sergio had wondered if Alex was gay for some time. As she watched him dancing, she wondered if "Love My Way" was his anthem too.

They entered the house.

Feeling guilty for intruding on Alex's private moment, she gave the door a good bang behind her. The music stopped immediately. Sergio disappeared upstairs to the bathroom, and she went into the kitchen to get a glass of water. Alex appeared in the doorway behind her. The poor lad had reached six feet at the age of thirteen. Now, at six four, his head almost touched the top of the door frame. She hoped to God he'd stopped growing, otherwise they'd have to get a bed especially made for him. People said he was a mix of her and Sergio. He had her long face and pale-blue eyes, and Sergio's olive complexion and winning smile. Recently, his face had been ravaged by a case of acne and he had taken to growing his dark hair long and parted in the middle, like a pair of curtains, which he hid behind.

Always an outgoing, lively child, Alex had retreated into himself when he was twelve or so. He'd stopped mixing with his peers, preferring to stay in and play on his Xbox, or watch football with his dad. Everyone was suddenly talking about teenagers and mental health, and Eileen wondered if he was depressed. Sergio said it was normal teenage behaviour but, looking back, she wondered if perhaps Alex was coming to terms with his sexuality then. Six months ago, when he started hanging out with Nathan and his gang, he had come out of his shell. Now he went out most weekends, was taking an interest in clothes and trainers, and he'd got himself a job at the local Tesco to pay for them.

Noticing his flushed cheeks and bloodshot eyes, she asked him if he'd been drinking.

He gave her a knowing smile. "I might have."

"Where did you go?"

He shrugged "Just out."

"With Nathan?"

He reddened and looked away.

"For feck's sake, don't let your dad find out."

Sergio had ripped the head off him after the meeting at the school. Laid-back to the point of horizontal by nature, he rarely lost his temper but that day he was incandescent. Pacing up and down the living room, he'd given Alex a history lesson on how members of his own family had disappeared at the hands of the Fascists, in the Spanish Civil War.

"And now my own son is attending rallies with fascists in this country?" he yelled. *"Those pigs are racists. They want people like us, your Spanish father and your Irish mother, to leave this country, but you have your photo taken with them?"*

Alex quivered with fear on the sofa. "How many times do I have to say it, Dad? I've said I'm sorry."

Sergio hovered over him. "I don't understand. You are a good kid. Tell me why you went to that rally."

"I don't know." Alex moaned and covered his face with his hands. "Because the others were going? Because it seemed a bit of a laugh?"

"A laugh? A laugh?" Sergio repeated at the top of his voice. Then he erupted into a stream of Spanish obscenities which Alex understood perfectly because he'd been bilingual from a young age.

"Enough, Sergio!" Eileen jumped up from the armchair where she'd been sitting in silence and shooed Alex out of the room.

She had her suspicions about why he had gone to the rally, but she wasn't sharing them with Sergio. Not yet, anyway.

Racist Scum Live Here. That's what the little gobshites had daubed on her wall. But Alex had never gone to that rally with a racist agenda. Of course he hadn't. Neither had he gone out of intellectual curiosity or for a bit of a lark, as he'd claimed. The more she'd probed him, the more it had dawned on her that he'd gone to impress Nathan. God love him, the poor boy was infatuated with him.

Michelle

Tony's snoring sounded like her old Range Rover cranking up. Michelle removed his tattooed arm from her bare breast as a rusty old pipe shuddered and groaned outside the grimy window. Still a little drunk, she could hear voices in the room next door. She hadn't realised the walls were so thin. She and Tony had made a lot of noise when they were having sex. Oh, the romance of a one-night stand in a Premier Inn in Ancoats!

Extricating herself gingerly from his other limbs, she slipped out of the bed, put her stockings and suspender belt in her bag and picked up her clothes from the four corners of the room. She dressed hastily. The sight of her forty-seven-year-old body in the full-length mirror made her wince: fried-egg breasts, ham-shank thighs, and hips the width of a prize heifer. She shook her head, and tutted. Some men would shag anything after two bottles of Pinot Grigio.

Earlier, in the wine bar, Tony had been kind, interested and funny. Despite the tattoos and laddish humour, she'd been attracted to him. So, when he'd offered her a line of coke, and asked if she wanted to get a room, she'd immediately said, "Why not?"

Clicking the hotel door closed carefully behind her, she slipped into her stilettoes, and hobbled down the corridor. The sex had been good, and she had no regrets. She'd been on dates with eighteen men from the app, ten of whom she'd slept with. She'd given them all ratings on her sexometer. Most scored below six, but Tony was the current winner to date, with an eight. Only one had asked her out on a second date and, as pleasant as he was, she knew that Tony wasn't going to either. She suspected that he was married and going home to a wife.

In the lift down to reception, she recalled a death-bed scene from a TV comedy she'd seen years ago. A grandmother was lying in bed, her granddaughter by her side.

"*Do you have any regrets, Granny?*" the young girl asked.

"*Just the one, pet.*"

"*What is that, Granny?*"

"*I didn't get half enough dick.*"

It made Michelle laugh out loud whenever she thought of it. Until recently, she hadn't had half enough dick in her life either. She had been nineteen and a virgin when she had met Rob and she'd been faithful throughout their thirty-odd-year marriage. Not so, Rob. When they divorced, on the grounds of his infidelity with

Jane, he confessed to sleeping with another eleven women. He was aghast when she said she hadn't strayed even once. Ever since, Michelle had been on a mission to sleep with lots of men to make up for lost time. Now, as she walked through the grubby hotel reception and into the chilly evening air, she was beginning to think that one-night stands were vastly overrated. What she really wanted was to find love again.

In the Uber on the way home, she texted Nathan to say she'd be back from her "book club" in twenty minutes. When he didn't reply, she assumed he'd gone out, despite being grounded after the meeting at the school. She mulled over the argument she'd had with Rob in the car park afterwards. That clueless tosspot had no idea how much his leaving had affected their boy.

It was a cold December evening with bruised purple skies when she and Rob had told Nathan they were splitting up. The blood draining from his beautiful face, he'd jumped up from the kitchen table and run out of the back door into the garden. When they'd looked out of the window, he was standing in the middle of the frosty lawn, his face pale with rage in the patio light. Above his head, he was holding the birdhouse. Her brother, Tommy, had made it for her, before he went to live in Australia, and she treasured it. Made of redwood, it had intricate leaf carvings along the roof, and her name etched on the handle. She'd often look at it and run her fingers along the carvings and think of Tommy and his family down under.

She banged on the window. "*No, please, Nathan, no!*" she screamed.

She and Rob rushed outside, but it was too late. Shards of wood were flying across the lawn and patio as he smashed it repeatedly onto the ground. As she watched, a terrible thought crossed her mind. If a clutch of baby birds were nesting inside, would he have destroyed it all the same? She was ashamed of that thought afterwards. He was fourteen years old, about to lose his dad, and hurting. Yet, it was interesting that he'd chosen to destroy something *she* loved so much, even though it was Rob who was leaving them for another woman.

Michelle had never understood Nathan's hero-worship of his dad. In Nathan's eyes, Rob could do no wrong. Yet, Rob had never been particularly affectionate or hands-on with Nathan when he was growing up. Neither did he spend much time with him. He was always working and, as Michelle later discovered, he was spending time with other women. At times Rob's indifference to his only son cut through her like a knife. Yet Nathan adored him, eagerly greeting him when he got in from work and following him around like a devoted puppy.

The one thing they did share was a passion for football and Manchester City. They had attended matches together since Nathan was very young and clearly some bonding went on there. To look at Rob now, you'd think he'd never done a day's exercise in his life but when he was a teenager he was actually a talented footballer who'd had trials with City. Nathan used to brag to his friends about his dad the footballer, spinning tall tales about all the star players Rob had met and the important matches he'd attended. Michelle felt that this, coupled with the lack of male role models in Nathan's life – he had no grandparents and only occasionally saw one uncle – led to him putting Rob on a pedestal he clearly didn't deserve.

Always wilful and difficult to control when he was a boy, from the day Rob left Nathan's behaviour had completely spiralled out of control. He started drinking and smoking weed soon afterwards. When he got caught with a spliff in the school toilets, she had to beg the Head not to exclude him, citing his excellent academic record and attendance. Then came a spate of shoplifting: an England rugby shirt from Next in the Arndale, sweets and alcohol from a shop in Chorlton precinct, and a bottle of L'Oréal foundation from Boots for a girl he fancied. It wasn't as if he didn't have the money, either. Rob's guilt over the divorce had landed Nathan a generous monthly allowance. Michelle suspected that Nathan was stealing purely for the thrill of it. He'd surpassed himself with this latest episode involving the Vote Leave rally, though. When she'd confronted him about it, he'd shown very little remorse.

The evening after the meeting at the school, Michelle had gone up to Nathan's bedroom. Shortly before he'd absconded to Spain with Jane, Rob had converted the attic for him. It had been intended as a teenage hideaway, where he could bring friends and girlfriends, but he'd brought hardly anyone back, preferring to loiter in shopping precincts and rain-sodden parks instead. The attic was a vast space with a sloping ceiling and beams, a table football, gaming chair, widescreen TV, and en-suite shower room.

She knocked and entered. Nathan was sprawled across his king-sized Man City duvet in his school uniform, watching something on his phone. Sometimes, she found herself staring at him and wondering if he'd been swapped at birth. She was a stubby, freckle-faced ginger, and Rob had a bulbous nose and F.A. Cup ears, yet they had somehow miraculously produced this beautiful boy. Six foot and muscular, he had white-blonde hair, perfectly symmetrical bone structure, and glacial blue eyes. Never in need of a brace, he also had a perfect set of Hollywood teeth. When he was younger, Eileen used to joke that he looked like a poster boy for the Hitler Youth, which was very disturbing in the light of his recent brush with right-wing extremism.

"What have I done now?" he asked when he saw the scowl on her face.

She gestured at him to take out his headphones. Then she sat down on the edge of his bed, told him about the meeting with the Head, how he'd been excluded for a week, and how his dad had behaved like a total dick. She also told him about the Prevent programme.

"What the fuck?" He threw his head back and laughed.

She thumped the bed. "It's not funny, Nathan. What in God's name were you thinking?"

Supressing a smile, he stared down at his phone.

She thumped the bed again. *"What the hell is wrong with you?"*

How she longed to snatch that phone from his hands and lob it out of the window. She was afraid to, though. The last time she'd confiscated it, he'd run away for twenty-four hours and she'd had to call the police. And, without it, she had no way of contacting him.

"Seriously, what on earth possessed you to go to that rally?" she asked. "I need to know."

He rolled his eyes and sighed. "I saw a poster advertising it, and a group of us went after school. I wanted to know what Vote Leave had to say about immigration and the referendum." He jabbed a forefinger at her. "You're the one always telling me to be intellectually curious and to question everything."

"But I never told you to attend rallies with Nazis and take selfies with them."

He ran his fingers through his hair. "I admit the photo opportunity was a bit dumb. I put it on a closed WhatsApp group, but some snitch got hold of it and spread it around."

"Have you any idea of the trouble you've caused?"

He said nothing.

"Did Alex tell you he got chased home from school by a gang of lads who graffitied his wall?"

He shrugged.

"You're all heart, Nathan Grainger. Alex is supposed to be your mate."

"I've told you before, he's not my friggin' mate. He just tags along with us."

She shook her head. "A far-right rally. That's not how you were brought up."

His eyes widened. "Excuse me? Dad votes UKIP."

"He also lives in Spain, and the export business he sold was made with the help of European funding. Don't you think that's a tad hypocritical?"

He replied with an icy stare. As a rule, she tried not to badmouth Rob, because she knew how much Nathan adored him.

She got up off the bed and left the room. She simply didn't have the energy to argue any more. While most of Nathan's misdemeanours could be put down to normal teenage rebellion, this recent incident made Michelle feel very uneasy. Did it hint at something sinister in his psyche? Or worse still, was he turning out like his dad?

CHAPTER 3

Eileen

Eileen parked in the drive and got out of the car. It had been a gloriously hot day and she'd spent it teaching seven hours in a stuffy classroom, followed by a two-hour meeting in an even stuffier staffroom.

Sergio had forgotten to put the grey bin out yet again. Cursing under her breath, she wheeled it out onto the pavement. She looked down at the low garden wall and winced. Despite scrubbing for hours, a few thin white streaks of paint remained. She glanced nervously up and down the street, wondering how many of the neighbours had seen what had been written there.

When she let herself in the front door, Rory was waiting in the hallway. He leapt at her, panting and slobbering, his tail going like a helicopter-blade. She dropped her bag and went into the tiny galley kitchen. Cursing again, she filled his empty water bowl from the tap, then watched him feverishly lap up its contents. She looked around. The feckin' state of the place! The dirty breakfast dishes and pans were piled up in the sink, the debris of a cereal packet was scattered on the floor, and she could smell dog-shite. She yanked open a window.

After finishing his last GCSE exam, Alex had gone on to his part-time job at Tesco, and she had been at work until eight in the evening. Sergio, on the other hand, had been at home sitting on the sofa scratching his arse all day, but hadn't lifted a finger to wash the breakfast dishes or give the dog a drink of water.

She marched into the living room, where he was sitting on the saggy orange sofa, surrounded by the clutter of his day: guitar propped up against the coffee table, half-full bottle of Rioja, overflowing ashtray, cigarette papers, and a half-filled-in job application form for an Amazon warehouse. Tinny modern jazz was playing on the turntable. She yanked the needle off the record and flopped into the battered leather armchair by the window.

"Would it not cross your mind to fill Rory's water bowl on a hot day like this?" she said. "The poor creature was dying of thirst."

Sergio rolled his eyes and reached into his jeans pocket. He took out a small bag of weed, picked up the cigarette papers from the table, and started to roll a joint on his knee.

Her eyes rested on the damp patch on the pale-blue wall above his head. It hovered like a grey cloud on a summer's day.

Sergio excelled at rolling spliffs. His other talents included charming women, playing classical guitar, and sex. Yet he never seemed to manage the mundane things her friends' husbands did, like navigating a computer program, holding down a steady job, or fixing a damp patch. She'd been making excuses for his unemployed status for years, especially to her family back home. It had happened just the other day on the phone when, for the millionth time, her mother asked if he had found a job yet.

"He's a classical guitarist, Mammy," Eileen had replied wearily. "It's hard for musicians to find regular work here, especially a Spaniard without any connections in the orchestra or theatre world."

"I know, sweetheart, and he's a fantastic musician. But, sure, *you* can't be carrying his dreams for the rest of your life." Eileen could hear the impatience and annoyance in her voice. "He's almost fifty years of age. He has to accept that he isn't getting a permanent job with the London Symphony Orchestra any time soon. It's time he got a proper job, any job, to help you pay the mortgage and the bills."

She was right, of course. Sergio needed to get a job. Yet, part of Eileen knew the only place Sergio truly belonged was up there on stage with his guitar. Not waiting tables, pulling pints, or pushing a trolley through an Amazon warehouse. The same way she belonged in a classroom. Watching him perform made her feel the same joy and pride she'd felt the first time she saw him almost thirty years ago. She'd been living in Spain and working in a bar in Estepona Port when he turned up with his cousin Toni to do a gig. She'd been mesmerised. When he made a beeline for her at the beach party afterwards, she'd been incredulous.

"I like Irish girls. They are always laughing," he'd said, as she hopped on the back of his moped at dawn.

The sun was rising over the sea on a golden horizon as they took the coastal road to her flat. He stayed that night, and never left.

She poured herself a glass of Rioja, sat back, and watched him tuck the tobacco deftly into the cigarette paper. His salt-and-pepper hair flopped over his dark eyes, as he rolled, licked and sealed, then tweaked the end of the spliff. She drank, the wine hitting her quickly on an empty stomach, the grouchiness of the day slipping off her, like a suit of tightfitting clothes.

Sergio patted the couch next to him. "Alex is on a late shift," he said with a grin.

"I know." Returning the smile, she put her glass down, went over, and stood in front of him.

Their fingers touched as she took the joint from him and raised it to her lips. She passed it back.

They locked eyes as she slowly peeled off her jeans and pants. She straddled him. They fed each other the joint and kissed some more. She traced the curve of his cheekbones, his stubble rough under her fingers. Her beautiful man. Sliding his forefinger along her breastbone, he hurriedly unbuttoned her shirt, and encircled her nipples under the lace of her bra. He was hard as she ground herself against him. She threw her head back and moaned. The sex was urgent and greedy, and they both came quickly.

Dozing off on the sofa afterwards, the dream came to her again. The renovated farmhouse with the whitewashed façade, Rory chasing chickens around a yard, the dark horse grazing in a nearby field. She was pinning sheets on a washing line on a windy day, Alex was sitting at a desk in an upstairs window, and Sergio was dressed in a tux and getting into a four-by-four with his guitar. Alex was always smiling in the dream, but Sergio never was. She woke up disoriented, not knowing where she was. Dream on, she told herself, when she was fully awake. House prices in County Mayo were scandalous. She wasn't moving back to Ireland any time soon.

As she cleaned up the kitchen afterwards, she beat herself up. She'd gone and done it again. Forgiving Sergio everything because he turned her on. Why hadn't he grown a beer belly and acquired a polished head, like most men approaching fifty? Instead, he'd aged like a fine Rioja. He was lithe, with a fecund head of hair, and his face was smooth, with only a smattering of laughter lines around his eyes. Women of all ages looked at him twice. She shook her head and swept up the scattered bits of cereal. Poor old Rory could have died of thirst today, but all it took was a look and a smile, and she was at Sergio like a bitch on heat. It really was about time she copped on.

Anne

The morning of Meg's long-awaited CAMHS appointment had finally arrived. Hakim had taken the day off work to accompany them to the clinic in town. Meg's mental-health issues and her subsequent school refusal had exploded into their family like a ten-ton bomb, leaving debris everywhere. They'd waited so long and today's appointment was a lifeline, a buoy they were clinging to, that could mark the start of her recovery.

Meg had sat her GCSE's at home, with an invigilator. Apart from a panic attack during one of her biology papers, she'd completed every single one. They'd been amazed at her resilience and terribly proud of how she'd coped. Now that all of that stress was out of the way, they'd hoped to relax for a while. No such luck. Meg was now fretting and losing sleep about how badly she'd done and, as the appointment date neared, she started panicking about that too. There really was no let-up. Meg's anxiety disorder reminded Anne of a wooden toy Meg had when she was a toddler. The aim of the game was to bang blocks of different shapes and colours into holes with a hammer. Whenever you succeeded in hammering one in, another popped up immediately afterwards. It was the same with Meg's condition. As soon as one worry was under control, another reared its ugly head. It was relentless and exhausting.

Every day Anne ruminated about the cause of Meg's problems. The previous four years, she had breezed through the school gates, in the top set in every subject, passing every exam with flying colours, and attending after-school clubs galore. Her teachers said she was a model student, with a solid group of friends. There were a few fallouts in the group in year ten, but nothing out of the ordinary for teenage girls. Then, at the start of her final year, Meg's behaviour went into a downward spiral.

At first, they were pleased that she was following the revision schedule Hakim had set out for her. The school had suggested two hours a night, but Hakim insisted she needed more. The following summer she was about to sit twenty-seven exams, and he thought two hours a night revision simply wasn't going to cut it so he suggested four. Anne went along with it, something they were very soon to regret.

In the weeks leading up to her mocks in November, Meg became obsessive. From the minute she got in the door after school, she got on her laptop and started to put in ridiculous hours, revising things that didn't need revising and asking for extra work to bring home. Her bedroom looked like a police crime-investigation scene, with revision cards all over the walls. She rarely took breaks, stopped going out with her friends, and started to shut herself away in her room. She even got up to revise on Christmas Day. Her eating habits became erratic, and she lost weight. Then, in early December, she started making excuses not to go in to school – stomach issues, headaches, and flu – God knows how many GP appointments she and Meg attended.

The day she was due to start back after Christmas, Anne found her in bed in her uniform, in the foetal position.

"I can't do it, Mummy," she sobbed. *"I can't do it anymore."*

The fizz of anxiety that had been slowly filling her brain had finally exploded, and she never went through the school gates again.

At first, Anne blamed herself. Were the Unbelievers right? Had she been over-protective of Meg? Had she failed to teach her resilience when she was young? After that, she threw the blame onto Hakim.

"You've always been obsessive about her education. You were the same with your other girls," she'd said to him, "Meg isn't as naturally bright as her sisters. She has to work hard to get good grades. Just because they all went to Russel Group universities and ended up with well-paid careers in accountancy and medicine doesn't mean Meg will. You've pushed her too hard. The poor girl is making herself ill because she's scared to let the side down."

Hakim was visibly hurt. "That's simply not true," he said. "I've always done everything in Meg's best interests. If you're looking for someone to blame for Meg's poor mental health, you might want to look closer to home."

Now it was her turn to be hurt. She'd walked away, stung that Hakim could be so cruel. He'd never once mentioned her father's problems before. She refused to speak to him for two days afterwards, pushing him away when he tried to apologise. Was he right, though? Were genetics the root of Meg's mental-health problems? Whenever Anne followed that line of thinking herself, she panicked, locked her thoughts away in the back of her mind, and threw away the key.

The appointment was at nine. They were all tired and grumpy, having been up late the night before, talking Meg down from her heightened state of panic.

She was sitting at the kitchen island, nibbling a croissant. Her left eyelid was twitching, a tic she'd recently developed that came on whenever she was stressed. She'd always looked young for her age, but her recent weight loss made her look eleven or twelve years old. A baggy sweatshirt hid her spindly arms, her bony knees poked through ripped jeans that had to be kept up with a belt, and her hair was tied back into a limp ponytail. She'd been such a beautiful child. She had stood out amongst her friends with her glossy waist-length hair the colour of melted tar, full lips, and Hakim's lovely amber eyes. Flat and indecipherable, they now stood out in her thin face like huge buttons.

When it was time to leave, Anne handed Meg her denim jacket.

She froze. "I can't do it," she said, covering her face with her hands.

"Of course you can, darling." Anne could feel her heart pounding. "We spoke about this last night. We'll both be by your side. You'll be fine."

Meg didn't move.

"Come on, put your coat on, sweetie," urged Hakim. "You don't even have to stay for the full hour if you don't want to."

She took her hands from her face and stared down at the table. "How can I explain to a stranger what's going on inside my head, when I don't even know myself?"

She snatched the jacket, put it over her head, and sat like that for the next twenty minutes. Now and again, she'd tighten the coat around her, like she was imprisoning herself inside a barbed-wire fence. No matter how much they pleaded and cajoled, they couldn't coax her out of her confinement.

Anne paced the room, watching the minutes tick by on the kitchen clock. She felt like the floor was caving in beneath her feet. Appointments with CAMHS were like gold dust, and this was their only shot at getting any real help. The thought of having to home-school Meg through her A Levels as well as her GCSE's was simply too much to bear. She would have to give up Clay Corner if that happened. Then, she'd go completely bonkers and need therapy herself.

Hakim asked her to give him time alone with Meg, so Anne left the room. When she returned, Meg still had the jacket over her head.

Anne looked at the clock one last time. "It's too late," she said wearily. "We've missed the appointment. You can come out from your hiding place now."

Meg slipped off the jacket, got down from the stool, and picked up her phone from the worktop. The sight of her leaving the room, casually scrolling, was too much for Anne, and the tension that had been simmering inside her for months boiled over.

"*You ungrateful little bitch!*" she yelled. "*We're doing everything to help you, but you're doing nothing to help yourself!*" She snatched the phone from her hand. "*And, until you do, you're not having this back!*"

With an astonishing amount of strength for someone so tiny, Meg pushed her back against the worktop, punching and scratching, and calling her all the names under the sun, as she tried to wrench the phone back. When Hakim finally pulled Meg off, she let out a bloodcurdling scream, grabbed a coffee mug from the draining board, and slammed it down on the tabletop, shattering the glass top into a thousand pieces.

Meg ran upstairs to her room, leaving Anne and Hakim staring in disbelief at the shattered glass. They had bought the table when they'd first moved in together. They'd fallen in love with the huge chunk of Indian railway sleeper bark encased in glass, along with the ornate carvings along the legs, and the glossy red oak.

Anne ran her fingers across the edge, tears running down her cheeks.

"Don't worry, darling." Hakim put an arm around her shoulders. "We can replace the glass."

"I know," she replied. "I just wished Meg could be fixed that easily."

CHAPTER 4

Eileen

Eileen, Anne and Michelle were sitting in the café in the Whitworth Art Gallery. The structure was a modern oblong extension made of glass and steel that had recently been added on to the old redbrick building. It overlooked Whitworth Park, a serene green space near the university area and an oasis in the busy city centre. Sitting in the café gave the sensation of being suspended, like being in a treehouse.

When the kids were small, Anne would organise outings to the gallery's Arts Workshops for children. Bored and restless, Nathan would dart around the hushed corridors with Michelle in pursuit, while Alex and Meg sat heads bent, sticking and gluing and painting, engrossed in the creative task at hand. Afterwards they'd eat a packed lunch at one of the picnic benches in the lush green grounds, dappled sunlight filtering through the trees. She, Anne and Michelle would have unfinished conversations, thoughts and words frequently interrupted by the kids, who would then rush off to explore the playground nearby. The giant hamster wheel was always a favourite – Meg, Nathan and Alex would spend ages in it, squealing and being thrown around like laundry in a washing machine, their laughter echoing like bells. They were joyous, jewels of moments, etched in her memory, of simpler, more innocent times.

She, Michelle and Anne were attending the opening night of an exhibition of one of Anne's sculptor friends. As they'd walked around the exhibits, Anne had enthused about the molten-glass pieces, explaining how they explored the concept of transparency and played with light.

Eileen found most modern art perplexing, but the way Anne had talked about it made it fascinating. Eileen noted how animated and upbeat she was, away from the tense situation at home with Meg. She'd been in tears on the way in when she'd told her and Michelle how Meg hadn't made it to her CAMHS appointment.

Michelle had looked bored with the exhibits and spent most of the time looking at her phone. "I didn't understand a word Anne was going on about," she'd whispered as the three of them made their way to the café for refreshments. "I'm only here for the free wine."

Eileen had laughed and called her a philistine.

Alex and Nathan had completed their exclusion from school without incident, there had been no further repercussions, and any bad feeling between her and Michelle had dissipated. Eileen was relieved. She hated any kind of conflict, especially with Michelle.

The three of them were sitting at a corner table with their complimentary glasses of Chardonnay. Outside the window, an eye-catching sign saying *Gathering of Strangers* hung on the gallery roof. It was made of multi-coloured neon and it stood out in the night sky. After a day of blue skies and sunshine, dark clouds were starting to gather.

Anne sipped her wine then cleared her throat. "Meg told me what happened with the boys at the school and the Vote Leave rally. Why didn't you tell me?"

Eileen and Michelle immediately lowered their eyes.

"I've been baring my soul to you about Meg's issues, but you kept *that* to yourselves?" Anne paused. "It's because Hakim and Meg are Muslim, isn't it, if not in the strict sense of the word?"

Eileen and Michelle nodded in unison.

"We felt so ashamed," said Eileen glumly.

"Really ashamed," said Michelle.

Anne sighed then squeezed both of their arms. "It was a stupid boyish prank," she said. "I love you both far too much to blame you personally for anything like that."

The sound of a plate smashing at the other end of the café near the bar made them jump. They looked over at the young distressed-looking waitress bending over the shattered pieces.

Lifting her glass, Anne turned to Michelle with an expectant look. "A little birdie told me you've been on another date."

Michelle shrugged. "There's not much to tell, really."

Anne wagged her forefinger from side to side. "I don't believe you."

"OK, then. He was called Tony, we drank a lot, did a few lines of coke then had loud sex in a Premier Inn in Ancoats."

Anne's eyes widened. "Honestly?"

Michelle nodded then Anne threw her head back and roared with laughter. "Darling, that's absolutely marvellous! And how did he score on the sexometer?"

"Eight."

Anne laughed again. "So I presume you'll be rebooking at the Premier Inn very soon?"

Michelle shook her head. "I'm pretty sure he's married."

Eileen reached for her glass. "For feck's sake, Michelle. Not another one. When are you going to find someone nice?"

"I just go for the ones who'll have me, Eileen. I'm a chubby, fifty-something, short-arsed ginger. They're hardly queueing up."

Eileen threw her a stern look. "You're a Titian-haired successful A&E consultant with a normal body weight who needs to work on her self-esteem."

"Here, here!" Anne raised her glass. "You're beautiful inside and out, Michelle. Don't settle. It's never too late to meet Mr. Right. I met my lovely Hakim at forty-one after a lifetime of catastrophic relationships."

Eileen recalled Anne once confiding that she'd once had to have therapy after a particularly bad break-up. She said she'd learned that she was fearful of committing herself fully to anyone, a fear that stemmed from the sudden death of the father she adored when she was in her teens. According to her therapist, in her mind her father had abandoned her, so every other man in her life would too. Soon afterwards she'd met Hakim. In Eileen's eyes they were as solid as a couple could be. Michelle's issues with men were different. Despite her outward appearance of being a strong professional woman who didn't give a toss what people thought about her, Michelle had very little sense of self-worth. When she looked in the mirror every day, she only saw ugliness, though she exuded beauty and strength. This lack of self-esteem led to dodgy choices when it came to men. Rob had treated her with disdain for years, and most men she'd dated since the divorce had treated her badly too. It baffled Eileen that someone so confident in every other walk of life could have so little faith in herself when it came to choosing a partner. She despaired at times.

Once, Michelle had told her that she'd been badly bullied at High School because of her red hair, glasses and swotty nature. She said she'd had very few friends the entire time she was there. Eileen often wondered if that was the root of her lack of self-worth. She had heard numerous stories of childhood bullying affecting people later in life. It was heart-breaking to think those feelings of worthlessness from her childhood had never left her.

The conversation moved away from Michelle's love life to the Brexit referendum which was about to take place in a few days' time.

Eileen was describing how much support she'd seen for the Vote Leave campaign around the estate. "I was leaving for work this morning and I spotted a Vote Leave campaigner coming down the path of George and Shirley's house opposite," she said. "He was only a young guy and he was wearing a T-shirt saying, '*We want our country back. Vote Leave on 23rd June*'."

Michelle gulped her wine. "Really?"

Eileen nodded. "George and Shirley were standing in the doorway behind him, smiling. Shirley waved at me, but a horrible uneasy feeling came over me and I wanted to run back into the house. It was feckin' awful. The thought that George and Shirley might be voting to get rid of the likes of me and Sergio sent a shiver down my spine."

Anne frowned and cleared her throat. "But it's not really the likes of you and Sergio the Brexiteers want to keep out, is it?" she said tentatively. "It's the hordes of illegals that are putting a strain on the schools and the NHS. You have to admit, it's nigh on impossible to get an appointment with a GP these days."

Eileen's eyes widened. "Hordes of illegals? What hordes of illegals?" She was taken aback. Previously, Anne had always been guarded whenever the topic of Brexit came up in conversation, but Eileen had no idea she had views like this.

Michelle picked up a coaster and cartwheeled it between her forefinger and thumb. "The NHS would collapse if it wasn't for its foreign workforce, Anne. Half of my team are EU citizens. To say nothing of all the Filipino, Indian and African doctors and nurses. And Irish too, of course."

Anne looked flustered. "Yes, of course. We need qualified people. I don't think limiting freedom of movement is a bad thing, that's all."

"Leaving the EU would be a disaster, especially for young people," said Eileen. "Take Meg. She's a talented linguist. If they limit freedom of movement, she might not be able to study languages at a foreign university or work in Europe because she doesn't have a European passport. Alex already has an Irish passport and Nathan can get one because of his grandparents so they'll be fine."

An awkward pause followed then Michelle leant forward and tapped Anne's arm. "You're not going to vote Leave, are you?"

She shook her head. "No, I'm not but I can understand those who are."

Michelle downed the last drops of wine from her glass. "I had a text from my cousin Seán in Donegal this morning. He lives close to the border. They're all crapping themselves about the border controls coming back."

Anne frowned. "I don't understand. Why would they need border controls?"

Michelle stared at her in disbelief. "Because if Brexit happens, southern Ireland would be in the EU and Northern Ireland wouldn't!"

Anne reddened. "Ah, I see."

Eileen sat back, scrutinising Anne's face. She began to feel the same unease she'd experienced the other day with George and Shirley, the feeling that she and Sergio were secretly viewed as 'other' by people she knew and liked. Except this was so much worse. Anne had been one of her best friends for years.

Shortly afterwards, Anne went to the other side of the room to greet a woman in black with horn-rimmed glasses, presumably her sculptor friend.

Michelle inched her chair closer to Eileen. "Is she for real? Does she really not understand what a vote for Brexit would mean for the Irish border?"

"She's not the only one. Loads of people I've spoken to don't have a clue. Teachers at college, educated people who should know better." She frowned. "Seriously, Michelle. If I thought for one minute that Anne was voting Leave, I'm not sure I could be her friend anymore."

"She's not voting Leave. Anyway, Remain are going to win by a mile."

"I really wouldn't be too sure about that."

Later, they walked through the park to the bus stop in an uncomfortable silence.

The air was moist after the heat of the day, and the breeze of earlier was picking up strength. Loose papers fluttered and empty cartons and cans rattled across their path. Storm clouds were gathering, grey-black and menacing, and the sky was tinged with yellow and green. The morning's forecast could be right. It looked like thunder and heavy rain were on their way.

Michelle

"You don't really believe any of that Vote Leave anti-immigration crap, do you?" Michelle leaned back against the kitchen worktop and watched Nathan wolf down the last of his Cornflakes from an enormous mixing bowl.

She had been reflecting on the conversation about Brexit with Anne at the exhibition the other evening, and Eileen's remark about the impact on their friendship if Anne was voting Leave. Up and down the country, families and friends were having heated debates like this and rifts were developing everywhere because of this stupid referendum. What the hell had that idiot David Cameron been thinking when he allowed it to go ahead?

Nathan shrugged. "Maybe I do think we're letting too many immigrants in. Maybe I don't."

"But your own grandparents were immigrants."

"So?"

"They were decent, hardworking people."

"I'm sure they were." He looked up at her. "And your Uncle Jimmy? Was he decent and hardworking too?"

Michelle stiffened, aware of his eyes boring through her.

Nathan grinned. "Dad told me all about him."

"I bet he bloody did."

Jumping up from the table, Nathan grabbed his blazer from the back of his chair, then ran upstairs without another word.

Michelle almost threw his bowl into the sink. She was raging. Uncle Jimmy was a secret, a part of her past she wanted to stay buried, and Rob knew that. How dare that fat spiteful git tell Nathan about him!

Taking a few deep breaths to calm herself, she took her phone from the pocket of her scrubs, logged on to Facebook, and brought up the picture of Nathan that she'd posted up on his sixteenth birthday. **"He's the spit of Jimmy at that age,"** her Aunt Teresa had written in the comments section below. Underneath that, Teresa had posted a grainy Polaroid of Michelle's dad and Uncle Jimmy in their teens. They were sitting on a wall outside the family home. Her dad had a protective arm around his kid brother, and they were both wearing coloured shirts under tank tops, and flares. Teresa was spot on. Nathan had an uncanny resemblance to Jimmy. Jimmy was skinnier, but they both had the same white-blonde hair, square jaw, high forehead and icy-blue eyes. There was something else too. Both looked at the camera with a similar air of defiance and fearlessness, like wild bullocks ready to charge. Michelle put her phone back in her pocket. She felt a twinge of guilt. Before her dad died, she'd promised him she'd visit Jimmy now and again, but she hadn't seen him in years.

When Jimmy was only a bit older than Nathan, he had done some very bad things – things that had ruined his life and cast a long shadow over her family. The repercussions made for a traumatic time in her childhood. She didn't like to think of those days and she locked the memories away in the back of her mind. In her darkest moments, she sometimes wondered if Nathan was heading down a path of self-destruction like Jimmy.

She could hear his heavy footsteps thundering down the stairs.

"*Turn on the news!*" Nathan yelled, slamming the front door behind him.

Michelle picked up the remote from the worktop and pointed it at the TV on the wall. She'd stayed up late watching the results come in, so she knew what was coming but she was filled with dread all the same. She clicked on the BBC News where an uneasy-looking David Dimbleby was shuffling papers and saying: "*The decision taken in 1975 by this country to join the common market has been reversed by this referendum to leave the EU. We are absolutely clear now that the Remain side cannot win.*"

Shortly afterwards, a puce-faced, delirious Nigel Farage appeared on the screen ranting on about the win being "*a victory for real people, a victory for decent people and a victory for ordinary people*".

She had been complacent, assuming Remain would win easily. Eileen hadn't. She'd had been right all along when she she'd said there was huge support for the Leave campaign. Seconds later, as if she knew she was thinking about her, Eileen sent her a text: "**Sergio and I are in bits,**" it said. "**If we could, we'd leave tomorrow.**"

PART TWO

CHAPTER 5

One year later

May 2017

Anne

Anne and Hakim watched Meg leave for the concert from the living-room window. She strode down the street with an air of new-found confidence, her long, glossy hair swishing from side to side, her legs and hips shapely now that she was eating properly again. She looked gorgeous in a denim mini-skirt, her new Convos, and the pink Ariana Grande T-shirt that her Aunt Hannah and her grandmother had sent from London for her seventeenth birthday.

Anne turned to Hakim. "I think we're finally getting our girl back," she said, smiling.

He nodded. "I do think you should let them make their own way home later, though. We said she needs to be more independent, remember?"

"I don't mind giving them a lift this once. The trams and buses will be crammed after the concert. I do take your point, though, darling. I need to let go more, now she's doing so well."

At the end of the previous summer, Meg had finally agreed to get help from CAMHS, where she was diagnosed with generalised anxiety disorder and depression. She'd been prescribed a low dose of anti-depressants and started regular counselling sessions. A reluctant patient, Meg was scathing about her therapist, Sonya, a woman in her fifties, with henna-red frizzy hair, tent-like floral skirts and emerald Doc Martens boots.

"Sonya hates me," she said. "I'm just another kid with problems, whose boxes she has to tick. At the end of every session, she asks me if I'm self-harming or have any suicidal thoughts. I think she secretly wants me to off myself."

That poor woman. Anne knew how impossible Meg could be.

At first, Anne wasn't sure about the meds. Meg seemed so young to be taking them. At sixteen, her brain still wasn't fully developed, and Anne had read scary stories online about addiction and the terrible side effects that could occur in teenagers. Ironically, suicidal thoughts seemed to be one of them. Meg was desperate to give the pills a go, though. It took a while to get the dosage right but, in the end, Anne had to concede that they worked. The dreadful panic attacks that Meg experienced subsided and the debilitating fizz that had prevented her from leading a normal life slowly started to calm down.

Meg insisted that it was the pills alone that had lifted her out of the dark place she'd inhabited for the past two years, but Anne suspected it was down to a mixture of things: the meds, the fact that she was more mature and more able to cope and, even though Meg wasn't admitting it, the talking therapy.

Anne also felt that leaving secondary school had a lot to do with it. The current education system put its children under so much duress. What other country in the world forced its sixteen-year-olds to sit twenty-seven exams in six weeks? Then there was the hysteria about attendance. It seemed to Anne that the system cared more school league tables and results than the wellbeing of its children. She was convinced it was making British children like Meg mentally ill.

Meg found studying for 'A' Levels much more manageable. Class sizes were smaller, contact hours less, she was studying subjects she liked, and she was part of a darling little friendship group, which included Alex.

Anne could finally go to work at Clay Corner every day, without feeling the need to check up on Meg every five minutes. Order and routine had been restored to family life, and she and Hakim could finally relax.

Oblivious to the extraordinary events about to unfold, Anne exited the Arndale car park, patted the back pocket of her jeans to check for her parking ticket and headed in the direction of Victoria Station. The concert was due to end at ten-thirty and she'd arranged to meet Meg and the others at ten forty-five by the taxi rank outside the station, a short walk from the Arena Stadium. It was a Thursday evening like any other. The night sky had an orange-and-yellow glow, there was a slow hum of traffic and a healthy trickle of people on the city streets.

As she approached Exchange Square, she looked around. She didn't get into town much these days but, whenever she did, she marvelled at how the city had changed since her arrival, almost forty years ago. She glanced up at the Vegas-like neon of the Printworks and the modern green-glass tower of Urbis close to the Gothic cathedral and the seventeenth century redbrick of Cheetham's College of Music. The old sitting comfortably next to the new. The imposing Corn Exchange across the road, once a meeting point for traders in the industrial revolution, was now a huge eating destination, and the outside area was humming with diners. She remembered when it was a large indoor marketplace, full of second-hand clothes and trinket stalls. She used to run one herself on the first floor, selling her pottery.

Raised in an elegant town house in Wimbledon Park, Anne had left London in 1987. When she told her family and friends that she wanted to study Fine Art at Manchester Polytechnic, they were horrified.

"But, darling, why on earth would you want to leave London?" her mother, Eleanor, had asked. "It's got the V&A and the National Gallery, but most importantly it's got Selfridges."

She chose to come to Manchester because it was her father Harry's birthplace. The son of an Ancoats grocer, he'd joined the army after school, met her mother on a tour of Germany in his mid-thirties, and they'd eventually settled in Wimbledon. Her sister Hannah had always been her mother's favourite, while Anne had always belonged to her father. His sudden death, when she was fourteen, had left her bereft and lonely. She'd lost not only a parent but an ally. She had headed to Manchester, her head filled with the sentimental notion that she'd feel at home in the place that had given the world her wonderful, clever father, but she'd been terribly disappointed.

She found a depressed city, with boarded-up shops, anti-Thatcher graffiti, dole-office queues that snaked all the way down the streets, and people who took umbrage at her accent. The poverty and anti-social behaviour in the high-rises close to her student accommodation in Hulme and Moss Side was a stark contrast to the well-to-do Wimbledon streets she was used to. It was all rather grim. But not as grim as the thought of returning to London and her mother, so she stayed.

As the years passed, Anne found a charm in the grey skies, dour humour and industrial skyline. Then, after the IRA bomb of '96, the city reinvented itself. A phoenix rose out of the ashes. Now, it was a young person's city, a tech hub brimming with shiny, high-rise city apartment blocks, populated by hipsters and artists who drank real ale in the trendy Northern Quarter, and frequented Home, the boho cinema arts complex.

"I hear Manchester's very up-and-coming," friends and family would say, whenever she was in London these days.

"Oh, yes," she'd reply, with a prickle of pride. "It's getting terribly swanky."

She walked on, wondering if Meg had enjoyed the concert and if she'd coped with the crowd. She recalled the text she'd received from Eileen earlier.

"Just to let you know. Nathan has a spare ticket so he's joining Meg and Alex tonight. Hope there's no drama. That boy seems to find trouble wherever he goes!!"

Poor Nathan. Eileen never had a good word to say about him ever since the Vote Leave rally episode the previous year. Granted, a photo shoot with the Far Right wasn't Nathan's finest moment, but Anne couldn't see why everyone had such a problem with him. He was very intelligent and perfectly charming whenever she met him. And he was terribly good-looking. She thought he looked like the twins from the 80's boy band Bros. She did find it a bit odd that he was going to an Ariana Grande concert, though. He was such a boy's boy, and Ariana was terribly girly. Nathan, Alex and Meg had grown up together. Unlike Eileen, she thought it was lovely that they were out socialising after all this time.

Suddenly feeling thirsty, Anne stopped by the tram stop in Exchange Square, took her water bottle from her bag, and raised it to her mouth. That was the moment she heard and felt it, a boom sounding like the loud bass of a drum. Her hand shook, the bottle missed her mouth, and a flood of cold water dripped down her chin. Passers-by stopped and cocked their heads to one side. Some exchanged anxious, expectant glances, as if they were waiting for something to happen.

She wiped her chin with the back of her hand. It could be anything, she told herself. A lorry backfiring, a sonic boom even.

You hear all kinds of sounds in the city. Putting her bottle back in her bag, she set off again. An uneasy feeling churned in her tummy. Whatever it was had felt close. Very close indeed.

Michelle

Michelle hadn't even been to bed with Billy O'Hagan, but she could tell he'd score a nine on the sexometer. The only thing preventing him getting a ten was the dodgy mustard Hawaiian shirt he'd worn on two out of their three dates. As the bell rang for last orders, she watched him saunter over to the bar.

Billy was a bear of a man with shoulders as broad and solid as a sturdy oak, and the kind of muscle that you could spot under clothing. He spoke with a soft Galway accent, his craggy face hinted at a life well-lived, and his eyes were a breath-taking cobalt blue. He lived in Chorlton with his fourteen-year-old son Will, and his daughter Bridget was in her first year at Glasgow University. Billy had been her last throw of the dice on the dating app, and Michelle had a feeling she'd bagged herself a winner.

It was their third date, and they were sitting in the back room of the Woodstock in Didsbury. Michelle liked the cosy feel of the pub, the oak beams, tatty leather chairs and sepia pictures of the local area on the walls. In winter, the smoky scent of a crackling open fire lured you in. She and Billy had been chatting about the relative merits of Didsbury and Chorlton. They both agreed that Didsbury was more up-market, with cleaner streets and more expensive houses, but that Chorlton had more of a hipster vibe, with more independent shops, vegan restaurants, and burglaries. Billy said his place had been done over twice.

As she waited for Billy to get served, Michelle rummaged in her bag for her phone. She was usually diligent about checking it, in case Nathan was up to no good, but she'd been enjoying herself so much that she hadn't looked at it all evening. Neither of them was drinking either. Billy was teetotal, and she was on an early shift the following morning. Despite the absence of alcohol, she was having the best laugh. Billy had a mischievous, dry sense of humour, and the banter and the craic had been batting to and fro across the table all night.

Michelle stared down at her phone screen, open-mouthed: five major incident alerts from the hospital, five missed calls from her colleague, Vicky, who was working that night, and one answer-machine message. She listened to the message. There'd been an incident at the Arena, Vicky said. A possible explosion, and the hospital was expecting a large number of casualties. She took a deep breath. A major alert was a case of all hands on deck.

Michelle knew she needed to get her arse in there immediately.

She put her phone down on the table, paused for a few seconds to think, then went into auto-pilot mode. By the time Billy arrived back at the table with their diet Cokes, she was heading for the door.

"Sorry. I've got to go in to work. Major incident at the Arena."

"Are you serious?" He gave her a concerned look, put the glasses down on the table, then followed her outside to the car park.

As they hurried past the rows of cars, Michelle was mentally preparing clinical areas and thinking about casualty numbers. Would they have enough staff? What about blood supplies? She'd almost forgotten she was on a date. Looking around for Billy, she saw him frowning down at his phone.

"What was on at the Arena?" she asked. "A gig?"

"Ariana Grande concert."

"Who?"

"American pop artist. Very popular with teeny- boppers. My Bridget used to be a fan."

"Teenyboppers?" Michelle closed her eyes and swallowed. "Jesus."

When they got to her battered Range Rover, Billy bent down and kissed her softly on the lips. "Thanks for a great evening," he said gently. "Look after yourself, now."

In the hours of horror that followed, the memory of his kiss, the touch of his stubble against her cheek and the smell of his apple-scented aftershave would keep her going. It gave her much-needed moments of respite, like a drowning person coming up for air.

Eileen

Glassy-eyed and stinking of weed, Sergio was standing over the bed shaking her awake. These days, he was smoking and drinking every night, and it was really getting on Eileen's wick. She'd gone to bed early, after a heavy teaching day and a run with Rory in the Meadows.

Sergio held out his phone to her. "Something's happened at the gig," he said nervously.

Yawning and pulling herself up on the pillows, she immediately thought of Nathan. What had he done now? Persuaded Alex and Meg to go to a dodgy club in town? Lured them into a crack den in Hulme? Nothing that little scut did would surprise her.

"Nathan doesn't like Ariana Grande, does he?" she'd asked Alex earlier when he told her that he was joining him and Meg at the concert. "I'd have thought he was more of a Kanya West type of guy."

"Now, now, Mother!" Alex had given gave her a mock scolding look.

She had searched his face for signs of the crush that she was convinced he had on Nathan in the past, but he'd turned away and was already hurrying out of the door.

Sergio's hand trembled as he handed her the phone. On the screen a BBC headline said: **Reports of Explosion at Manchester Arena**.

Eileen felt the breath leave her. She handed back the phone then tugged her own from its charger by the bed. There were three missed calls from Anne who was supposed to be giving the kids a lift back from the concert. She sat on the edge of the bed and called her back, but the call went to voicemail.

She then called Alex and the same thing happened.

"I'm going into town to find him," she said, jumping up and pulling on a sweatshirt and her jeans. She pushed past Sergio, who was slumped on the bed, drunkenly navigating his phone. She went to the toilet.

Afterwards, when she went downstairs, Sergio was waiting by the front door in his leather jacket, holding out the car keys.

"I'm coming with you," he said, enunciating his words carefully and steadying himself on his feet, in an attempt to look sober.

"No, you're not. Someone needs to be here when Alex comes home." She pulled on her trainers, snatched the keys from his hand, and pushed him out of the way. "Keep your phone on, and for Christ's sake do *not* fall asleep."

As she reached for the door latch, she looked back at him in disgust. "The feckin' state of you. You're never there when we need you, Sergio. *Never.*"

Slamming the door behind her, she hurried to the car in tears.

It was true. She'd never been able to rely on Sergio in a crisis, and tonight was no exception. She could never relax whenever she left Alex with him when he was young, always worried he'd have one spliff or one drink too many. He forgot to pick him up from school multiple times, and when Alex was three he lost him in Morrisons supermarket. A friend of theirs found him wandering in the car park. Sergio never said a word to her about it. She'd had to find out from the friend.

She got into the car, wiped her eyes, and banged her fist on the steering wheel. Christ, how she hated him right now for making her face this alone! She took her phone out and looked at the

Manchester Evening News website. The emergency services were telling everyone to stay away from Victoria Station and the area around the Arena. But how could she? Her boy was out there. Every tissue of her being was telling her to go and find him.

She set off, driving through the empty Chorlton streets towards Stretford, then turning onto Chester Road, the main dual carriageway into town. She decided she'd park in one of the side streets on Deansgate, then walk in the direction of the Arena as the streets nearby might be cordoned off. She put her foot down, picking up her phone from the passenger seat at regular intervals and trying Alex's number.

As she neared town, police cars, fire engines and ambulances whizzed by. Terrible thoughts invaded her head, each one edging the other out of the way. Alex and Meg were responsible kids. If Alex's phone had died, he'd have borrowed one and called her. So why hadn't he? Oh God, where was he? She'd never considered Manchester a safe city. She always worried whenever Alex went out in town. Crime levels were high, and there was always trouble in the city centre at night. She couldn't believe this was happening. She should have moved back to Ireland years ago.

Waiting at the traffic lights at Deansgate, Eileen thought she saw a plume of smoke billowing over the skyline ahead. Or was it simply a cloud? On a billboard to her right, a boy of about ten was advertising Nike football boots. Dark-haired, olive-skinned and sitting on a football, he reminded her of Alex in his football-obsessed days. He and Nathan would trudge around a muddy field at Hough End Juniors every Sunday morning, barely ever winning a game. Once, Sergio had got tickets to see Real Madrid play against Utd at Old Trafford. Alex had barely slept the night before. They'd found him at six in the morning, waiting in the kitchen wearing his Real Madrid kit and scarf, ready for the match. What an uncomplicated, happy-go-lucky boy he was back then! There were endless birthday parties and playdates involving *Minecraft* and *Star Wars*, Then, in his early teens, the difficult years arrived. That was when the sudden growth spurt made him exceptionally tall and he withdrew into his shell. Uncomfortable in his new skin, he walked around with hunched shoulders, like he was carrying the weight of the world.

One of the kids Alex knew from Chorlton High, Sara, had recently transitioned to become Sam. Eileen had bumped into his mum recently who'd told her that Sam and Alex had been going to some of the pubs in the gay village in town. Eileen had found a crumpled-up flyer in Alex's jeans pocket one morning, when she was doing his laundry. A leather-clad man, smiling behind a music deck against a background of rainbow colours, was advertising Resident DJ nights in a club in Canal Street. Alex must know that she and Sergio had no issues with him being gay. She'd dropped enough hints. Yet he still hadn't come out to them. Why didn't he want to tell them? All she wanted was to put her arms around him, squeeze him tight, and tell him everything was fine. And now? What if something bad had happened to him, and he'd never told them who he really was? She fought back tears at the thought.

Halfway down Deansgate, she turned into a side street near Kendall's and found a parking space. She made her way to the High

Street, looking down at her phone as she walked. She still couldn't get through to Anne or Alex, but there were texts and missed calls from family and friends in Ireland and Spain. Sergio must have told them Alex was at the concert. The fecking eejit. She knew as much about Alex's whereabouts as they did. The last thing she needed was a barrage of calls and texts when he might be trying to get through to her. She clicked on the *Manchester Evening News* website. It said that parents and unaccompanied children who'd been at the concert were gathering at the Park Inn Hotel so she decided to head there. As she was searching Google maps to find the route, her phone rang. Anne's name came up on the screen. Her hand shaking, Eileen answered.

Anne

When Anne arrived at the top of the road that led down to Victoria Station, she stopped in her tracks. British Transport Police in black-and-yellow high-vis uniforms were swarming everywhere. Officers were cordoning off the exit with duct tape and gesturing at people to move away from the building. The Arena stadium was directly behind the station and connected by a short walkway which was used by concertgoers to get to transport links. Only one black cab stood at the rank where she'd arranged to meet Meg and the others. The rest were being driven away.

A few metres away, a woman in a white puffa jacket and enormous hooped earrings was shouting into a phone with a diamante-encrusted cover.

"*I don't fucking know, do I?*" she yelled. "*I've only just got here! She said something about a shooter, but I couldn't hear because of the screaming in the background! Someone here said something about a bomb!*"

Anne felt all the muscles in her body stiffen. She took her phone from her bag and called Meg's number. It went straight to answerphone. Meg often didn't answer her calls, so she didn't panic. Looking up, she saw a group of concertgoers in pink Stetsons and glittery T-shirts hurrying out of the station. An older woman was hunched over the group of young girls, like she was shielding them from heavy rain. Behind them another group of young friends, clutching hands, suddenly broke into a run as soon as they got through the exit. The sight made Anne freeze. She began to feel numb and detached, like she was watching everything happening around her on a TV screen.

She rang Meg again, this time holding the phone with both hands, because they were shaking so much.

"Pick up, darling!" she said, again and again, but there was no reply.

Her legs about to buckle, she hurried across the road to the grass area by the Urbis building. She sat down and waited. Other parents and family members started to arrive, worry and disbelief etched on their faces. They reminded her of Anthony Gormley's lonely cast-iron statues on Crosby beach, but instead of looking out to sea they had their eyes fixed on the station entrance. Some had their heads dipped into their phones. A bald man nearby who had been trying to contact his granddaughter told her the signals had gone down. She gripped her phone tight, the way she used to hold on to Meg's hand in crowded places when she was little. Like a magpie drawn to precious stones, she scrutinised the station exit for Meg's long, glossy hair and shiny pink T-shirt. She rang her number over and over, then rang Hakim but she got no reply from him either.

She looked up at the bright night sky. *"Please, God,"* she begged, *"not again. Please, don't let this happen to me again."*

A minute or so later, as if someone out there had been listening, her phone rang. The first thing she heard on the end of the line were the screams of young girls. It was a sound that would never leave her. Years later, if she was relaxing in a hotel pool or walking through the local park, the high-pitched shrieks of children would invariably make her stop what she was doing and transport her back to that moment.

"Meg?" Her voice was small and hopeful.

After what seemed like an age, she heard Nathan's voice on the end of the line.

Michelle

Before she set off, Michelle checked the BBC website. It said the explosion had happened just after ten-thirty and there were unconfirmed rumours of casualties. Someone inside the Arena had caught the sound of the blast on phone footage. She hesitated before clicking on the video. Pink balloons filled the screen, and young girls were screaming and jumping over seats in a panic, trying to escape the seating area. She turned it off, a knot tightening in the pit of her stomach. The A&E department in the Children's Hospital would get the brunt of the casualties. They would get the rest. She cursed when she realised her phone was running out of juice, then cursed again when she realised she hadn't brought a charger. She quickly texted Nathan to say she wouldn't be back tonight. He'd told her earlier that he was going out in Chorlton. Whatever he was up to, at least she could console herself that he was nowhere near the terrible events unfolding in town.

Some of the roads into town were blocked and the satnav took her a longer route to the hospital. When she arrived, she parked up close to the main entrance. Getting out of the car, she looked around. She could only see one ambulance. Where were they? The hospital was only a five-minute drive from the Arena, ten at most. She hurried inside to the staff reporting area, feeling a tug of hope. Maybe the casualty numbers weren't as high as feared.

Ten minutes later, she was pulling on clean scrubs in her designated cubicle. Joel, a Portuguese nurse she'd worked with many times, was filling a container with plastic gloves beside her. She liked Joel. He had bundles of energy, lots of interesting body art, and a friendly, assuring manner with the patients. He'd been about to go home after his day shift but had stayed when the major incident had been declared. They'd lost a lot of foreign nurses after Brexit. Thank God for the good ones like Joel who'd stayed.

"You OK?" she asked, as she washed her hands in the sink.

He chewed on a pierced lip. "I never worked on a major incident before."

"Me neither, pet." She dried her hands with a paper towel then patted his back. "You'll be fine. You know, I didn't even know who this Ariana Grande was."

He threw her a look of mock horror. "You don't know Ariana?"

"Nope."

"Where you been, lady?" He shook his head, wiggled his hips, then sang a line of a song, something about a dangerous woman.

Michelle smiled.

"Ariana's the best!" he said, turning to put a clean paper roll on the bed.

Minutes later, they were treating the first casualties. Most of her experience had been with trauma, not blast wounds, and now she was suddenly dealing with shrapnel injuries on a scale she'd never seen. The bomb had been filled with nuts and bolts, to inflict maximum injury. Shrapnel flew at a body at speed, and destroyed everything in its path, damaging tissue, blood vessels, muscles, nerves, and bone. Each nut and bolt was a weapon in its own right.

She and Joel spent the next six hours diligently picking metal from the flesh of youngsters. One girl's neck was peppered. Mia was seventeen, in shock and babbling. Michelle had to ask her to stop talking, as she prised the shards from her skin.

Mia clutched Joel's hand. "Ariana was brilliant," she kept saying. She had a dusting of gold glitter on her eyelids. Michelle pictured her laughing and dabbing it on in her bedroom with her friends, hours earlier.

The night went on, and the victims kept coming. Michelle marvelled at how calm many of them were. Few cried out in pain or made demands. One man in his sixties had got caught up in the blast when he was waiting to pick up his granddaughter. He told Michelle she was a hero. As he was being wheeled into surgery, he grabbed hold of her hand and kissed it, but she'd looked away.

As the hours ticked by, she was hearing stories of victims being left with no medical aid for over an hour after the bomb went off. She was starting to sense that something had gone badly wrong with the emergency services' response. Heroes they were not.

Shortly after two in the morning, they lost an eighteen-year-old in an adjacent cubicle. Grace looked like a girl in a pre-Raphaelite painting, with alabaster skin and waist-length copper hair. She had lost a lot of blood quickly, after substantial chest and leg injuries. The ambulance was a minute or so away when she went into cardiac arrest. Andy, a young paramedic Michelle knew well, had accompanied her in. She spotted him in the corridor after the girl passed, thumping the palm of his hand against a wall. She was about to go over and comfort him, but one of the porters got there first. Grace's family arrived ten minutes later.

Michelle took a break around three o'clock. In need of fresh air, she headed for a nearby courtyard. She sat on a bench with a coffee and stared at the pink petals on a nearby rose bush, lit up in the moonlight. In all her years as a doctor, she'd never experienced anything like this. She struggled to process the enormity of it. Had someone really filled a bomb with nuts and bolts and detonated it at a concert full of kids?

She hurried back along the main corridor, now a warzone, lined with distraught parents and teenage girls being comforted by nurses and paramedics. Back in the cubicle, Joel told her that they'd had been told to bag all the shrapnel for evidence. As they placed the metal shards in the correct bags, she wondered how many other medical staff were doing the same in emergency rooms all over the city. She quickly banished the thought to the back of her mind. She had no time to dwell on the number of casualties and the dead.

Half an hour or so later, Alison, a Senior A&E nurse, put her head around the cubicle curtain.

"Got a wee minute, Michelle?" she asked tentatively, in her throaty Glaswegian accent.

Michelle stepped outside.

"I just spoke to Elaine further along in cubicle ten. Your son's here. He's absolutely fine but he's asking for you."

"What?"

"Nathan, isn't it?"

Michelle's heart thudded. She nodded, then stepped back into the room where Joel was filling out the last patient's paperwork.

"My son's here," she said, peeling off her gloves and tossing them in the bin. "Apparently he's fine but I need to check what's going on. I'll be back in a few minutes."

Without waiting for an answer, she left and hurried along the corridor.

CHAPTER 6

Six weeks later

July 2017

Michelle

Rob was sitting at the breakfast bar, shovelling down last night's leftover lasagne from the fridge. She hadn't seen him since his Oscar-worthy tantrum at Chorlton High, fifteen months before. It seemed such a long time ago. So much had happened since.

He had come to whisk Nathan off to Marbella for three weeks. Michelle couldn't wait. Twenty-one whole days without cleaning up his shit, being rudely awoken by the bang of the front door at two in the morning and putting up with his scowls and sulks whenever Billy came over. A wide grin spread across her face as she pictured Jane picking up Nathan's dirty pants and towels from the marble bathroom floor in the villa, and Rob being woken by phone calls in the early hours demanding lifts home from parties.

"That was my tea, Piggy," she said, entering the room.

Without replying, Rob wiped his fat chops with a piece of kitchen roll. Throughout their marriage, he'd teased her about her weight, singing a song called "Hey, Fatty Bum Bum" to her on a regular basis, and calling her names like Thunder Thighs. Now, he was the porker, and she was relatively slim. She'd lost weight after the stress of the divorce, then she'd enrolled at a gym to keep it off. She'd lost a bit more when she met Billy. Being around him made her lose her appetite like a love-struck teenager.

She threw Rob a filthy look and yanked open the dishwasher door. "You can't just swan around here like Lord of the Manor and help yourself to the contents of the fridge!" she snapped.

"Strictly speaking, it still is my manor. Half of it, anyway." He eyed her slyly. "Maybe we should think about selling up."

Michelle turned away and bit her bottom lip. They'd agreed not to sell, at least until Nathan had left university. Rob knew how much she loved this house. They'd bought it not long after they got married when it was a ramshackle shell with a damp problem, a leaking roof, and dodgy electrical wiring. Unbeknownst to them, Chorlton was about to transform from gritty inner-city suburb to fashionable bohemian enclave. Trendy bars, restaurants and trinket shops would soon open on every corner, and property prices would soar. Michelle was oblivious to any of that, though. She'd simply fallen in love with the house. Tucked into a cosy corner of Chorltonville, overlooking the Meadows, it had turrets, winding garden paths, and small, arched, stained-glass windows. It reminded her of the house in "Hansel and Gretel". She'd grown up on the council estate on the other side of the tracks. Never in her wildest dreams did she think she'd own a house in Chorltonville. When their offer was accepted, it really was the stuff of fairy tales. Rob had never made any noises about selling up until now. She was hoping to buy him out one day. She was planning on leaving the house in a box.

She snatched the plate from under his nose. "You'll have to get an Uber to the airport," she said.

"I thought you were giving us a lift."

"I'm busy."

"Got a date with Billy Boy, have we?"

"None of your business."

"Nathan's told me all about him." Rob stuck his fingernail between his front teeth and rummaged.

She waited for an obnoxious comment or a putdown, but instead he nodded and said, "I'm happy for you. Really, Michelle. I am."

She started to unload the dishwasher. Then, a few seconds later Nathan bounded into the room, his face brightening the second he saw Rob.

Despite the copious amounts of alcohol and drugs he was consuming these days, Nathan looked a picture of health and vitality. His eyes were bright, his skin clear and tanned, his hair had grown and was now chin-length and bleached even lighter by the sun. In his cut-offs and white T-shirt, he looked like a surfer dude.

"How's my hero?" Rob lumbered off his stool, grabbed Nathan in a headlock, and ruffled his hair. "I've been telling everyone in Spain how my son saved his friend's life at the Arena bombing."

A spot of play-fighting followed. Laughing, Nathan wriggled free, then headed to the fridge, and took out a can of Coke.

"Did you see they've arrested the bomber's brother in Tripoli?" he said. "I reckon they'll arrest the rest of his family any minute now."

Rob shook his head. "Towelhead scum!"

Michelle slammed knives and forks into the cutlery drawer. "Language like that is *not* helpful," she said.

"Language like that is far too good for them!" Rob sat down on the sofa. "This country gave Abedi's family asylum, and they paid us back by killing our kids."

Michelle turned her face to the window and gripped the worktop. In the reflection of the glass, she could see Rob giving Nathan a high-five. She hated the way he fuelled Nathan's anger about the bombing. She was furious about it too, but there were better ways to deal with it than stoking up further hatred. There were still nights when she woke up in a cold sweat reliving it all, the bolts and shards of metal in young skin, the desperate faces of worried parents, then the shock of Nathan and Meg turning up like that.

After Alison, the senior nurse, had passed on the message that Nathan was in another cubicle, she hurried down the corridor to find out why. He'd told her he was going out in Chorlton, so what the fuck was he doing here?

Meg was lying on the bed in the cubicle. Nathan was sitting next to her, without a mark on him. Relief washed over her like a cool breeze on a sweltering day. They'd been holding hands, but quickly pulled apart when she appeared. The left-hand side of Meg's beautiful face was red and swollen, and her right arm was bandaged. Scratches and angry red bruises were scattered along her skinny arms, neck, and legs.

Michelle had the strongest urge to pull Nathan to his feet and hold him tight but she hesitated. He was at that age when he shrugged off shows of public affection, especially in front of friends. She stepped towards him, rubbed his back and asked him if he was OK.

He nodded, unable to meet her gaze. "Sorry, Mum," he said. "I should have told you I was going to the concert. Meg had a spare ticket. It was a last-minute thing." He looked shaken up and, for a change, vulnerable. "I did try to ring you when we got here, but I assumed you'd be busy."

"You could say that." She smiled weakly. "My phone was out of charge, so I wouldn't have seen your call anyway."

For once, she was thankful for his thoughtlessness. She could never have done her job properly if she'd known he was out there caught up in it all.

"It was bat-shit crazy," he said. "People were saying there was a shooter, and everyone started screaming and running for the exit."

"I tripped," said Meg. "People started trampling all over me."

In her relief at seeing that Nathan was OK, Michelle had almost forgotten about Meg. She was such a frail-looking little thing anyway but, with her cuts and bruises, wide scared eyes and masses of dishevelled hair, she looked like a rag doll that had been stamped on by a cruel child.

"Nathan rescued me," she said. "He pulled people off me and saved me."

"He did?" Michelle slowly felt herself glow with pride.

She picked up Meg's notes and flicked through them. She'd sensed Nathan watching her since she got there, as if he'd just realised what she did for a living, like she was more than the person who did his washing, tidied up after him, and made his meals every day.

Meg's injuries weren't serious. They would heal quickly, but Michelle wondered about the mental scarring. The poor girl already had issues. How on earth was she going to cope with the trauma of all this?

She sat down on the edge of the bed and asked Meg if they'd given her anything for the pain. She nodded, tears brimming in her big dark eyes.

Michelle squeezed her healthy hand. "I assume you've contacted your mum?"

"She's on her way here," Meg started to sob, "but we still haven't heard from Alex."

"Alex?" Michelle frowned. "Alex was at the concert with you?"

"He left early," said Nathan quietly.

"Why?"

They exchanged a look, but neither spoke.

Meg wiped her eyes. "We've been trying his phone all night, but the line is dead."

Michelle was trying to process it all. "Does Eileen know?"

Meg nodded. "Mum said she's gone into town to look for him."

Michelle's heart contracted. Alex was missing, and Eileen was out there searching for him. She glanced up at the wall clock, her thoughts returning to Joel on his own in the cubicle and the patients waiting outside.

She got up off the bed. "I have to get back. Don't worry, guys. Alex will be absolutely fine." She tried to sound matter-of-fact. "He's probably at home or stuck on a tram somewhere."

As she stepped towards the door, Nathan inched his chair closer to the bed. When she'd seen them holding hands earlier, she'd thought of it as a comforting gesture. Now she wondered if it was something more.

She hurried back to her cubicle. She could see Joel at the end of the corridor, waving frantically and wheeling a new patient in. She was still thinking about Eileen searching the city for Alex when she spotted Hilary, one of the girls who worked on reception, coming out of the staff bathroom. Michelle ran over to her, gave her Alex's name and description, and asked if he could check with all the hospitals, to see if he had been brought in. It wasn't much, but for the moment it was all she could do.

When the Uber to the airport arrived, Michelle grabbed Nathan and hugged him hard. Ever since the bombing she'd made a point of being more affectionate with him even if he did shrug her off a lot of the time. Twenty-two people died that night, most of them young, the youngest eight years old. Over a hundred were injured and hundreds more left mentally scarred. Every morning, she woke up bursting with gratitude that he had escaped unscathed. She was giving him the odd hug whether he liked it or not.

When Rob and Nathan had gone, she texted Billy and told him to come over. After showering, she put on the new pale-blue summer dress she'd bought online, poured herself a glass of Chardonnay and put Christy Moore on the sound system. The late evening sun warmed her face as she sprawled on the sofa by the window. Her negative thoughts about Rob and her memories of the bombing slowly began to fade. Spending time with Billy always made everything so much better.

Anne

Anne shook the tartan blanket and spread it at the foot of a large oak. It was a stinging hot day on Turn Moss playing fields and the sun hung high in a cloudless sky. A Sunday football match had just ended nearby and young female players in green-and-white-hooped jerseys trooped past on their way to the car park, red-faced and sweating in the heat.

Minutes later she spotted Michelle bounding across the lush field towards her in a khaki top and denim cut-offs. She was swinging an M&S carrier bag by her side. She looked relaxed and happy, probably because Nathan had left for Spain a couple of days previously and she was now spending some quality time with Billy. Michelle deserved it. They all deserved good things after what they'd been through these past six weeks.

Inspired by the weather forecast, Anne had called Michelle and Eileen the day before and suggested a picnic. She wasn't sure Eileen would make it. Neither she nor Michelle had seen her since the day after the bombing when the three of them had sat in her kitchen, shell-shocked and trying to process what had happened. She had bailed out of a number of arrangements since then because she was dealing with Alex. Meg and Nathan had been so lucky. Poor, darling Alex less so. Anne still caught her breath whenever she thought about the moment she found him that night.

She'd been waiting, sitting on the grass area opposite Victoria station, ringing Meg on a loop and losing her mind, when Nathan finally answered the phone.

"We're looking for a taxi to take us to the Infirmary," he'd said. "Meg got trampled on in the rush to get out. It doesn't look like she's got any serious injuries, but she needs to get checked out."

Anne felt the stranglehold on her neck loosen and she was finally able to breathe again.

"I'll join you at the Infirmary," she said.

He put Meg on the line.

"I'm OK, Mummy. I'm a bit battered but I'm OK," she said, between sobs. "We can't contact Alex. He left the concert early and he's not answering his phone."

Anne steadied her voice and tried to keep calm. "Don't worry, darling. The phone signals keep going down, that's why. Alex has probably made his way home."

"I love you," Meg said and ended the call.

Her voice was so tiny and weak, Anne thought her heart might crack in two.

She later learned that the bomb had gone off in the foyer outside the seating area but the noise and impact of the blast had unleashed total panic and chaos everywhere. Terrified concert-goers started leaping over seats and running for the exits, causing a stampede. Meg and Nathan were among them, but Meg had slipped and fallen. As she disappeared under the crush, Nathan had fought his way through the trampling feet and dragged her out without a thought to his own safety. When they finally got outside, they couldn't find any medical help at hand, so Nathan had carried Meg through the streets until he found a taxi to take her to the Infirmary. Whatever anyone said about that boy ever again, he would always be a hero in her eyes.

Anne had called Hakim and left him a message saying Meg was safe – he'd gone to bed early and slept blissfully through the whole thing. Then she'd called Eileen, who was on her way into town to look for Alex. When Anne told her that he'd got separated from

Meg and Nathan, she heard the distress in her voice that she herself had felt only minutes before, that raw primeval fear that your child is in danger. Anne felt conflicted. While she wanted more than anything to stay and help Eileen look for Alex, her need to get to the Infirmary to be with Meg was stronger.

Shaken up and dazed, Anne stood up and brushed herself down. The roads all over town would be chaotic and many would be closed off so she decided to leave the car and walk to the Infirmary. It wasn't far. As she was about to head off, she heard shouting across the road. A burly, bald man, presumably a parent, was trying to push past a British Transport officer to get into the station area. He was shouting that his daughter was in there. Anne averted her gaze from his distress, her eyes travelling over the far side of the grass area.

And there was Alex. He was sitting down, half hidden by a couple of waiting parents. It was definitely him. She'd know those gangly limbs and straggly hair anywhere. He had come to the taxi rank as arranged before they left for the concert. Glued to her phone, she had missed him.

She hurried over to him, calling out his name, but he didn't seem to hear. He was hunched over, his long arms draped loosely over his knees, his hair falling around his face. From a distance, he looked crumpled, like a runner who'd collapsed after a race. As she approached, she could see he was covered from head to toe with a thick layer of dust. His hair looked like he was greying prematurely, and his jeans and white T-shirt had a metallic sheen. His eyes were staring straight ahead, and his face was streaked with dirt.

Startled, he looked up at her, then gave her a small nod of recognition.

She lowered herself to the ground and sat beside him. "It's OK, sweetie, it's me, Anne," she said.

She put a hand on his arm, but he shrank from her touch. More shouting erupted at the station entrance, and he placed his hand over his right knee, to steady the shaking.

She racked her brains, trying to remember the First Aid Training she'd learned when she was a teacher. What was it they said about treating shock victims? Something about reassuring the victim and keeping them warm.

"It's OK, darling, you're safe," she said. "Everything's going to be fine."

She took off her jacket and placed it over his wide bony shoulders, but it was way too small, and slipped off.

"Alex – can you tell me if you're injured or hurting anywhere?"

He didn't reply.

"Do you have your phone with you?"

He continued to stare ahead into the distance.

"We need to get you checked out. I'm going to try and get you some help, but you mustn't move, OK?"

She stood up and looked around at the enfolding scene of chaos. Groups of fraught concertgoers were emerging everywhere, parents' phone calls were becoming more frantic, and more and more people were arriving, including a TV film crew. She searched for an ambulance or a paramedic but couldn't see any anywhere.

Taking out her phone, she called Eileen.

"I have Alex," she said. "We're on the grass area opposite Victoria Station. He's in shock, but he's safe. I'll wait here with him until you get here."

After a short silence, they both burst into tears.

Now, even today's sunshine couldn't obliterate the memories of that night.

Eileen arrived at Turn Moss half an hour after Anne and Michelle got there. Her pale face was hidden behind a floppy straw hat, and she looked super-slender in a black floral wraparound dress. The three of them sat cross-legged in the shade of the large oak, drinking Prosecco from paper cups and eating prawn and avocado salad, falafel and hummus. They chatted generally for a while, she and Michelle waiting patiently for Eileen to open up about what was going on with Alex.

Anne uncrossed her legs and leant back against the trunk of the tree. "Meg's suddenly started going out all the time. I found a bag of weed in her jacket pocket last night," she said. "She fell through the door at two. I waited until she was asleep then tiptoed downstairs and rummaged through her pockets. That's when I found it."

"Really?" Michelle's eyes widened. "Are you sure it was hers?"

Anne nodded. "Pretty sure. I've seen the signs before. I've smelled it on her clothes and she empties the contents of the fridge some nights, which is unusual as she's such a picky eater. She'd been sleeping lots as well."

"They're all at it these days." Michelle dug her plastic fork into a prawn. "It's so easy to get hold of."

"Hakim will go bonkers if he finds out. I doubt Nadia, Aisha, or Farah ever had a puff of a spliff in their lives. I'm certainly not going to grass Meg up. She and Hakim are at loggerheads enough as it is."

"Does Meg know you found it?" asked Eileen.

Anne shook her head. "I was going to flush it down the loo, but I felt such a hypocrite. I smoked my fair share of spliffs when I was much younger than Meg. Weed was rife at my all-girls school in the 80's and I was mad for it. I did it to help me block out the trauma of my father's death. Meg's probably using it to block things out too."

"You mean the bombing?" Eileen had repositioned herself and was lying on her side, her long arm bent, her face resting on her hand.

Anne nodded. "That, plus she's probably using it help quell her anxiety in general. To numb the fear and slow down her racing thoughts. I worry, though. Some people, especially those with mental-health issues shouldn't go anywhere near drugs. When I was sixteen, Virginia McKay, my classmate in St Joan's, ended up on the psychiatric ward in Tooting Bec after a bad trip on weed. She went from being deputy head girl to thinking she was married to Terry Hall from The Specials and being followed by MI5. Rumour has it that she joined the Quakers."

"Virginia McKay sounds great," said Michelle, laughing and reaching for a strawberry. "I wouldn't worry. I'm sure smoking the odd spliff won't do Meg any harm."

Anne sipped her Prosecco. "Things could be so much worse. I was dreading the fallout of the bombing. I was fully expecting her to decide that the world was too terrifying to live in again and for her to retreat to her room. But she hasn't."

Anne glanced over at Eileen who was gazing out over the fields. She could have kicked herself. Why was she going on about how well Meg was doing when it was obvious Alex was suffering badly from PTSD? You bloody idiot, she said to herself. It must have sounded like gloating.

As if she knew what Anne was thinking, Eileen said, "I'm happy Meg is coping so well. You were worried she'd never go near a crowded place again, but she's been amazing, going to the One Love concert and doing all that fundraising in aid of the victims. You should be proud of her resilience."

"*Aw*, thank you, sweetie. We are very proud."

Michelle pulled the cork from a second bottle of Prosecco with a confident twist. "Nathan is obsessed with the bomber and his family," she said, pouring the fizz into their waiting cups. "It's hard to believe Abedi lived only a mile away in Fallowfield. I haven't told you but in the days after he was caught Nathan cycled up to the address quite a few times. He came back buzzing with stories of armed police, helicopters, and raids on nearby houses. The police chased him away for taking pictures and videos."

"Are you serious?" Eileen raised her cup to her lips.

"I'm worried about him. One night he left his laptop open on the kitchen table and I searched his history. He's been going on dodgy right-wing websites and commenting on forums, like he's some kind of expert on terrorism. He's totally obsessed. He brings every conversation back to the topic of the bombing and the bomber. Rob fuels it all. I've heard him spouting anti-Islamic crap on their Skype calls. I could kill him."

Anne swirled the Prosecco in her cup. "Have you talked to Nathan about it?"

"Loads of times. I've pleaded with him to stay away from the online hate and suggested he lay flowers in St. Anne's Square for the victims instead. I've told him again and again that you can't blame an entire Muslim community for the wrongdoing of a couple of individuals."

"What did he say?" asked Anne.

Michelle sighed and slipped her sunglasses from the top of her head onto her face. "He said 'It's not just a couple of individuals, though, is it, Mum? There are cells operating out there, and the terrorists need to be weeded out'."

Anne plucked at the grass at the edge of the blanket, "Maybe it's his way of coping. Everyone deals with trauma differently."

Eileen cleared her throat. "Alex was so lucky. I can't believe how close we came to losing him."

Anne and Michelle immediately turned their faces towards her and gave her all their attention.

"It doesn't bear thinking about," said Anne. "How is he doing? Is he sleeping better?"

"A bit, but he still gets flashbacks and nightmares."

"Is the trauma therapy working?"

"Hard to tell, really. It takes time. At least he's agreed to come to Ireland with us."

Michelle sat up. "That's brilliant. The break will do him the world of good."

"I hope so." Eileen seemed reluctant to say more, so they didn't press her.

Later, the three of walked home through the long grass with flushed faces and a sway in their steps. The sun was moving closer to the horizon, casting a honey-coloured hue over the fields, and there was a hum of crickets.

Anne stepped towards Eileen. "Did Alex ever tell you why he left the concert early?" she asked tentatively. "Meg's been cagey about it whenever I've asked."

Eileen frowned and looked ahead. "He hasn't told me, but I've got a pretty good idea."

Anne and Michelle craned their necks, looking at her expectantly, but she said nothing more. Instead, she walked on ahead, leaving a trail of silence in her wake.

CHAPTER 7

August 2017

Eileen

The spate of good weather continued into August. Skies of uninterrupted blue, temperatures in the mid-twenties, and not a drop of rain since they'd got off the ferry in Dublin. Everyone they met in the village said they'd brought the good weather with them.

Eileen had been woken early that morning by the call of a cormorant outside her old bedroom. She got out of bed and inhaled the view. Cobalt-blue skies were dotted with light cauliflower-shaped clouds and lush emerald fields sloped down to the winding road bordered by rich reds of heather and gorse. The craggy outline of the mountains was clear, and the lake glittered like topaz.

In all her years away, she had clung to the memory of the view from her bedroom window like a keepsake. As she trudged the grey Manchester streets, she often closed her eyes and pictured it in her mind's eye. As her longing to return home to Mayo intensified, the view became more than a mere recollection – it was a visceral yearning for the landscape, like an insatiable thirst on a boiling hot day. After each visit home, she was more and more reluctant to return to Manchester. Brexit had only intensified the feeling. A year on, the hurt, rejection and anger she'd experienced on the day the UK exited the EU were as raw as ever.

Sunlight flooded through the windows of the kitchen in Glencorrib, illuminating the picture of the Pope and the framed blessing next to it about the road rising up to meet you and the wind being always at your back. Despite her father Dermot being a builder and her mother Bridie nagging him, the house hadn't been updated in years. The paint on the walls was faded and peeling and every room was filled with red pine furniture. Dressers, tables, chairs and wardrobes, all identical. Eileen reckoned there must be an entire forest contained within those walls.

Eileen and her younger sister Nicky were in the kitchen. Nicky was carefully peeling the cellophane from a platter of salmon and cream-cheese canapés. People often remarked on how different they looked and how they found it hard to believe they were sisters. A bottle-blonde, with a heart-shaped face, Nicky had curves and was a normal height. Today, she was dolled up in a pink flouncy dress and matching heels, with a pair of Jackie-O sunglasses glued to her head even though she hadn't been outside the door since she arrived.

Nicky had notions. Lots of them. Before the twins, Luke and Mikey, were born, she had worked in marketing for the Irish Tourist Board. She'd had a walk-in wardrobe, a collection of Paul Costello suits and her colour coordinated blouses and handbags were all displayed on the shelves like works of art. The boys were ten now, and Nicky didn't need to work, thanks to her husband Paul's income as a solicitor in the town. Luke and Mikey rampaged around the house in crisp white shirts and shiny black pants, their hair gelled back like small mobsters. Eileen had watched them all get out of the Jeep earlier, wondering if they'd come straight from Mass or popped into a wedding on the way.

Nicky had always been the more organised and efficient sister. Today, as well as the canapés, she'd brought along a Greek salad and a tray of home-made brownies. She reached up to open a cupboard door, throwing a disdainful glance at Eileen's sad offering of a Centra carrier bag full of crisps and nuts.

Eileen pulled a face. "I'm not feckin' cooking. I'm on holiday."

"You can do the washing-up, so," Nicky replied with a smile that didn't quite reach her perfectly made-up eyes.

When Nicky turned away, Eileen gave her sister the middle finger. She was still raging with her for what she had said about Sergio that morning.

Eileen had walked over the fields to Nicky's house to spend some time with the boys. Nicky and Paul lived in an enormous new build with five bedrooms, a long gravel drive and ornate pillars on either side of remote-controlled gates. Inside, the walls were all beige, with black-and-white portraits of the family everywhere, along with signs saying, *Love, Live, Life* and other nonsensical quotes.

The house was showroom tidy and clean. You'd never know two boisterous boys lived there. Even the cushions on their beds were lined up at an angle on their Manchester United duvets.

Eileen arrived at the back door unnoticed. She was about to take off her walking boots when she heard her da's voice through an open window. She could see him drinking tea at the kitchen island. Nicky was folding Brown Thomas towels and placing them in a white wicker basket. Both had their backs to her.

"Sure, what can I do?" he was saying. "He needs the papers to stay in the country. To think he's lived over there for nearly twenty years and now he has to fork out for citizenship papers. What a shower of bastards!"

Nicky held up a towel to check for stains. "Let Sergio get a proper job to pay for his own citizenship papers. You're too good to them, Da. You're always bailing them out."

"Didn't I bail you and Paul out once, so you could hold on to this place? That cost a lot more than Sergio's citizenship papers."

Nicky sniffed. "Ah, now, that wasn't our fault. That was the banking crisis."

"All I know is that Brexit isn't going to make it any easier for Sergio to get a job now, either."

"Brexit, my arse!" Nicky threw a towel into the basket. "Sergio doesn't want to work. He's nothing but a feckin' waster!"

Eileen froze. At that moment, she hated her sister more than anyone in the world, even Michael Gove.

Furious, she turned around and ran through the vast garden, past the enormous trampoline and made her way back to

Glencorrib. If anyone was to call Sergio a waster, it would be herself, not her lazy bitch of a sister, who hadn't done a day's work in ten years. Nicky was nothing but a trophy wife with a crooked lawyer husband.

Yet, as hurt as she was, hearing Nicky say those things about Sergio was no big surprise. She had always viewed him like he was about to steal her Dolce Gabbana purse. It was Da she was more upset with. Why would he go and tell Nicky he had helped them out? Eileen felt betrayed. She was surprised to feel herself suddenly well up. Having to ask Da for the money to help with his citizenship papers on top of all that had been yet another humiliation. She trudged through the fields, the sun hot on her back, vowing never to ask him for another penny as long as she lived.

Nicky swirled into the front room, canapés in hand, Eileen following with her bottle of Coors and bowl of Taytos. Paul and Da were sitting on one sofa in their green-and-red Mayo jerseys, roaring at the big screen, where Mayo was losing to Galway in the GAA derby. Luke and Mikey were sitting on the floor with bottles of Orangina and Sergio was perched on the other sofa with her cousin Shannon. Sergio was nursing a glass of Rioja. Mammy had made a big show of telling everyone how she'd got it especially for him, as if bottles of Spanish wine were like gold dust in the big Tesco.

Sergio was watching the match, bemused. In all his years coming to Ireland, he still couldn't get used to seeing players on a football field handling the ball as well as kicking it.

Eileen squeezed onto the sofa between Sergio and Shannon, who was home from New York on a flying visit with her sixteen-year-old daughter Madison, a cool-looking kid with blonde-tinted dreadlocks, oversized trousers, and a velvety New York accent. She and Alex had spent most of the afternoon upstairs together playing on the Xbox.

Growing up as cousins, Eileen and Shannon had been close. Born four months apart, they were raised a mile away from each other. They'd gone on to study at UCD together, sharing a ramshackle townhouse behind Grafton Street with three other girls, a tortoise and a one-eyed cat. A med student, Shannon was hell-bent on moving to New York. As soon as her green card came through, she begged Eileen to join her, but Eileen didn't want to follow what she saw was the hackneyed path of Irish emigration to the States. As part of her degree in modern languages, she'd spent six sun-filled months in Malaga on the Erasmus programme and was desperate to return to Spain. It simply didn't occur to either of them to stay in Ireland. They were part of the "brain drain", the swathes of young graduates who had left the country in the 80's. Despite an ocean and a time zone between them, over the years she and Shannon had kept in touch, graduating from letters to email, to cheap transatlantic phone calls, then texts, and now Skype.

America had been good to Shannon. Now Senior Consultant Paediatrician in a hospital in Long Island, she owned a waterfront townhouse in fashionable Freeport, a boat, a docking bay, and a quayside condo in Florida. She had recently split up with her wife, Denise, an African American doctor. Madison had been conceived by a donor, Shannon had carried her, and she and Denise shared custody.

As a girl, Shannon had been a willowy beauty, with inky, waist-length hair. Now, it was pure grey and cropped close to her head. Her pale Irish skin had been weather-beaten by the hot New York summers, and she was a little overweight. Despite the divorce, she seemed happy in her own skin and content with life. Eileen envied her.

The match over, Eileen passed the bowl of Taytos around. It was yet another loss for Mayo. Mammy and Aunt Peggy, Shannon's mother, appeared in the doorway at the final whistle, high-fiving each other, and shouting, "*Up Galway!*" They'd been born and raised in Salthill.

Da was sitting with his arms folded on top of his paunch, shaking his head. He looked broken. "If we got rid of the shirt-lifter in goal," he said, "we might've be in with a chance."

Paul reached for his bottle of Coors. "That bender is no bloody good. He's cack-handed."

A hushed silence fell over the room.

"For fuck's sake," said Shannon, getting up from the sofa and heading for the door.

"No offence, like," said Paul, as she passed him.

The goalkeeper they were referring to had recently come out, and his story had been all over the tabloids.

Da was red-faced and staring down at the floor. Mammy stepped towards him. "Ya feckin' eejit!" she said, slapping the top of his bald head.

Eileen's heart sank. Only a few days before, she'd told her parents that Alex was gay.

"You can't help who you love," Da had said but now here he was, flippant, homophobic comments rolling easily off his tongue.

Eileen followed Shannon outside. They sat down on the low wall at the front of the house overlooking the lake, beer bottles in hand.

Shannon shook her head, looking glum. "Are you sure you want to come back and live here?" she said. "I sometimes wonder if this place has changed at all in the last thirty years."

"Don't take any heed of Da and Paul. That's only macho GAA talk. Attitudes here are a lot more liberal than you think."

"You sure about that?"

Eileen swatted a wasp from her face and frowned. "Yes, I am. You only come back every now and again, Shannon. You don't see the changes. It isn't a land ruled by priests and nuns wielding big sticks anymore. It's a very different country from the one we left behind."

"I hope so. For Alex's sake. Anyway, how's he doing? Is the therapy working?"

Eileen shrugged. "It finished last week. We only got six sessions on the NHS."

Shannon balanced her bottle on the wall. "We can help out, if you need more. Pay me back. Whenever."

Eileen shook her head and blushed. First Da, now Shannon offering her money. She was quickly becoming the family charity case.

"Is he able to talk about it yet? To his friends?"

"He doesn't see anyone as he won't go out. Meg's been round a couple of times, but not so much now that she and Nathan are an item."

"Nathan's the boy Alex had a crush on?

Eileen nodded. "From something he said, I've got a feeling he left the concert early because he saw Nathan and Meg getting together."

"Oh, man! Then he walked right into the bomb."

"It's just a hunch." Eileen sighed. "I feckin' hate Nathan. He's still a kid, and his mother is my best friend, but I can't help it. He leaves a trail of destruction everywhere he goes. He probably knew Alex had a crush on him, but he still had to get off with Meg in front of him."

"Why do they all fall for him? From what you've told me he sounds like a narcissist in the making."

"He is, but like a lot of narcissists he's beautiful and charming when the mood takes him." Eileen shook her head. "Meg's parents have no idea they're together."

"Really?"

"Hakim doesn't like Nathan either. He'd be livid. Anne wouldn't mind, though. She thinks the sun shines out of his behind because he saved Meg from being trampled on in the rush to get out of the Arena."

"And what does Michelle think?"

Eileen shaded her eyes from the sun. "I haven't a clue. I've hardly seen her lately. She's with her new fella all the time."

"You sound pissed with her ... I mean mad."

"A bit. She hardly ever texts or asks how Alex is doing. Anne's been a godsend, though. She knows all about kids and mental health because she's been through it with Meg. It's been hell, Shannon. It really has."

Alex didn't speak for two whole days after the bombing. He didn't sleep properly for weeks, afraid that his dreams would transport him back to that night. About a week in, he started to talk about what happened.

"I remember being lifted off the floor and thrown forwards," he said. "Then everything went quiet. I lay there for a bit. When I got to my feet, it was foggy everywhere and my eyes were clogged with dust. People were moaning and screaming and calling for help. I wiped my eyes ..." He started to tap his right foot, a tic he'd developed.

Eileen took his hand in hers. "It's OK, take your time."

"That's when I saw the bodies and the bits of bodies. One or two were kids, like seven or eight years old. My T-shirt and jeans felt damp. I thought it was blood and I'd been shot or something. I stumbled around for a bit, then I staggered towards the light and made my way outside. It was total chaos. Everyone was shouting and screaming and running in all directions. I remembered we were meeting Anne at the taxi rank by the station to get a lift home, so I headed there. It was like my brain wasn't connected and my legs had a mind of their own. I just kept going."

He started to cry, and she held him.

When they pulled apart, he wiped his eyes and said, "You and Dad know I'm gay, right?"

She nodded. "We do, sweetheart."

"I thought so."

She held him again, tighter this time, her heart bursting with gratitude because he was alive. "We both love you so very much."

So there, after all the waiting, he'd come out to her.

Sergio fought back tears when she told him that evening. She panicked at first, thinking he had a problem with it.

"I'm not upset because our son is gay," he said. "I'm upset because he is suffering. I feel useless. I am his father, and yet I cannot fix any of it."

Eileen and Shannon went back into the house. She could hear Luke and Mikey, shouting excitedly in the back garden.

Nicky popped her head around the kitchen door. "Quick!" she gushed. "Paul and Da got hold of some fireworks for the boys. They were supposed to be for the Mayo win, but he's letting them off anyway."

Eileen froze. *Dear God, no!* She ran through the kitchen into the back garden, but it was too late. A sudden crackle filled the air followed by an explosion and a hiss and another crackle. Cheers erupted and she yelled at them to stop, but Da was already after lighting another.

She found Alex upstairs crouched in the corner of her old bedroom. A helpless-looking Madison was hovering close by. Alex had his hands over his ears and was rocking back and forth, emitting low moans, like an animal in pain. She went to him, wondering if the things he saw that day would ever go away. Could he ever unsee them, or would they be burned into his brain forever?

PART THREE

CHAPTER 8

Ten months later

June 2018

Michelle

Michelle glanced at the door for the umpteenth time, then looked down at her watch.

"They're teenagers." Billy leaned over the table and squeezed her arm. "Sure, they're never on time for anything."

"Nathan's doing this on purpose."

Billy cocked his head to one side. "It might be genetic. You wouldn't be the best timekeeper in the world yourself."

"Cheeky!" She laughed and slapped his arm playfully.

The Bowling Green pub was busy. Known locally as the Bowler, it was nestled next to the site of an old church and graveyard near Chorltonville and was one of the few remaining Irish pubs in Chorlton. The menu offered bacon and cabbage, a decent Irish stew, and regular GAA football and hurling matches were shown on the big screens.

Nathan had just turned eighteen, and she and Billy were meeting him and Meg for his birthday lunch. Michelle had offered to pay for a party somewhere (no way was she sacrificing her house to fifty marauding eighteen-year-olds), but Nathan wasn't interested, saying he'd prefer to go clubbing in town with Meg and his friends instead.

Kevin, the jovial owner of the Bowler, hurried past with his hands full of glasses. He smiled, gave them both a "Howiya", then headed for the bar. Kevin was from Limerick and an old friend of Billy's from back in his drinking days.

Early on in their relationship, Billy had confided to Michelle that he was an alcoholic. He said he'd also had issues with drugs when he was younger. She'd always suspected a wild past. You don't get that many lines on your face from early nights and daily yoga. She imagined he'd bedded scores of women as well, but she didn't like to ask about that. Other women might have scarpered at the revelation of his addictions, but it was too late for Michelle. She had already fallen for him big-time.

He said that he got sober the day his wife Julie died, three years before.

"If I'd touched one more drop after that day, I'd never have stopped," he said. "And then who'd be around to care for my wee ones?"

There was nothing wee about his son, Will. At fourteen, he was tall and sturdy like his dad and a talented rugby player. The poor lad clearly hadn't got over losing his mum. He walked around trailed by a shadow of sadness. His sister Bridget was the same, except that her grief came out as anger. Freckle-faced, with long flame-coloured hair and multiple piercings, she permanently looked like she wanted to give everyone a good kicking, and she wore big, twelve-hole Doc Martens that suggested she might. Bridget had self-harmed after her mum died, and the scars were still visible all the way up her thin, pale arms. Michelle only ever saw her briefly in the holidays when she was home from university. Bridget was wary of her, in the same way that Nathan was wary of Billy. Neither of them wanted a replacement parent for the one they'd lost.

Billy rarely spoke about Julie, so Michelle didn't prod or poke. Like her, Julie was second-generation Irish Mancunian. She'd died at forty-two of inflammatory breast cancer, one of the most aggressive types of the disease. Once, at Billy's house, Michelle had picked up a photo of Julie from the mantelpiece. A bit tipsy at the time, she'd said, "Julie looks like me. Have you got a thing for short chubby gingers, or what?"

Mortified, she slapped her hand over her mouth. How could she have been so disrespectful?

To her relief, Billy had laughed and said, "That's just the type of comment Julie would have made."

Taking the photo from her hands, he looked at it tenderly for such a long time that it put a damper on the rest of her evening.

A dreadlocked young waitress, with a blue gemstone in her nose, arrived at their table to collect glasses. She was wearing a yellow T-shirt emblazoned with a picture of the Manchester Bee and the words: *22nd May 2017. Never Forget.*

First used as a symbol of the city during the Industrial revolution, the bee symbol gained popularity after the bombing. It had come to represent the strength, solidarity and community pride that was shown in the face of the tragedy. The bee was everywhere, in murals all around the city, on bags and tattoos, and in every Mancunian's heart.

In her role as first responder, Michelle had attended the one-year anniversary ceremony of the bombing in the Town Hall, two weeks before. Sitting in that stuffy function room with politicians, minor celebrities, and the victims' families, she'd felt a myriad of emotions: unspeakable sadness for the family members, pride in the way her city had responded, and survivor's guilt because Nathan had escaped, when all those other kids hadn't. Rumours were circulating about mistakes made by the organisations in charge – the slow response of the emergency services, the transport police who hadn't patrolled the area where the device had been set off, and the intelligence services who'd failed to monitor the bomber, even though he was known to them. The thought that the bombing might have been prevented made Michelle feel sick to her core.

Cartwheeling a beer mat between her finger and thumb, she glanced at the door yet again. Where the hell were Nathan and Meg? She and Billy had been together for over a year now, but Nathan was still full of resentment towards him. Billy rarely stayed over at the house, as he couldn't leave Will on his own but, when he did, Nathan made sure he wasn't welcome. He played loud music, scowled in Billy's presence, and refused to partake in conversation with either of them. It was a ridiculous situation and Michelle had decided to do something about it. The meal was meant to be an attempt to smooth things over, but now she was beginning to wonder if Nathan and Meg were even going to show up.

She watched Billy saunter over to the bar, his denim shirt taut across his broad shoulders, his hips slender in black jeans. She thought about the sex they'd have later, his hands and tongue exploring every inch of her, and the weight of him as she wrapped herself around him. Unlike Rob, Billy was a selfless, considerate lover. Yet, when they were having sex, she'd catch him off guard sometimes, looking at her quizzically, like he was searching for something he'd lost. He was probably asking himself what he was doing with someone as pug-ugly as her. She knew deep down that he was way out of her league and could have any woman he wanted. Michelle was convinced that she only had him on loan, until someone younger and prettier came along.

Pink-faced, giddy and forty minutes late, Meg and Nathan finally burst through the door. Michelle gave them a tight smile as they slid into the seats opposite, then she thrust the menu at Nathan.

"Billy's at the bar. Hurry up and decide what you want."

She took their orders then joined Billy.

"I think they've already been drinking," she whispered.

He glanced over at the table. "Of course they have. It's a Saturday night and they're eighteen years old."

Their faces lit up when Billy placed two pints of Stella on the table in front of them, instead of the two halves she'd asked for. She watched Nathan lap his up, like a dog drinking from his bowl on a hot day. He'd put on weight recently, especially around the face, probably the result of all the takeaways and beers consumed when Meg stayed over to 'revise' for their A levels. Where he was getting the money to pay for it all, she had no idea. Despite all her nagging, he still didn't have a job.

From what Michelle could gather, Nathan and Meg had been together on and off since the night of the bombing. They seemed happy enough. Meg brought out Nathan's caring side which, it had to be said, hadn't had much of an airing for a while. The way he was around her reminded Michelle of the way he used to be around his pet hamster Cheeky, when he was a boy. He lavished more time, love, and attention on that rodent than on any of his friends, and he was heartbroken when Cheeky passed. Meg was no sick pet, of course, but she was a delicate soul, and it was touching to see how loving and protective he was around her. Since they'd got together, Nathan seemed to have left all that crazy Islamophobia and right-wing nonsense behind him too. These days, he even argued with Rob about his support for Trump. If he only he could be nice to Billy, life would be perfect.

Meg smiled sweetly at her. She'd recently developed an emo look. Her large eyes were heavily lined with kohl, complete with another layer of pink underneath, and her foundation was deathly pale. She'd cropped her lovely long hair short and dyed it electric blue. Michelle thought it made her look cheap. Today she looked waif-like in a black mini-dress, fishnet tights and pointy ankle boots. Nathan had more of a 'jock' look. He wore colourful rugby jerseys, jeans, and trainers. Together they made an incongruous couple.

"I see City got a hammering at Chelsea today," said Billy. A lifelong Utd supporter, he gave Nathan a teasing grin.

Nathan responded with a filthy look but Billy ploughed on, undeterred. With Bridget for a daughter, he was well-versed in the ways of stroppy teens.

"Do you get to many matches?" he asked.

"Not anymore. I did when my dad was around." He frowned at Michelle. "He had a company box at the Etihad, and we had season tickets. He had trials for City when he was young. He nearly made it."

"Cool," said Billy.

Michelle turned to Meg. "Are you doing anything nice for your birthday next week?" she asked in an overly cheerful voice.

"Hakim has invited me over for the day," said Nathan. "Me and him are going to play charades, drink champagne, and have a good old chinwag, aren't we, babe?"

Meg dissolved into a fit of giggles that continued for some time. Nathan joined in. Michelle looked quizzically at Billy. What was so funny? Had she missed something? Yet, despite Nathan's jokey bravado, there was hurt in his eyes. He and Meg had kept their relationship secret from Anne and Hakim for months. Anne was fine about it when she found out, but Hakim made it clear to everyone involved that he wasn't one bit happy. He didn't want his daughter anywhere near Nathan, even if he had saved her life at the Arena.

Nathan attacked his burger and chips, and Meg picked at her lasagne. Michelle was disappointed at how quiet she was throughout the meal. She was usually very chatty when she came over to the house but now she seemed more interested in the cockapoo lying under the next table. She kept moving her head from side to side and staring at it, like she'd never seen a dog in her life before. It was all very odd.

Billy kept the conversation afloat with comical anecdotes from his teenage days in Galway. He had them all laughing, even Nathan. The conversation turned to A Level grades and universities. The previous summer, Nathan announced out of the blue that he wanted to study medicine. Michelle had been gobsmacked. He'd chosen to study three sciences at A level, but he'd never shown a bit of interest in medicine before. He surprised her even further by working hard and doing well in November in his BMAT exam, an admissions test for med school. Now he had offers from three universities.

Meg looked at Nathan adoringly. "We both want to go to Liverpool," she said.

Nathan wiped his plate with his last chip and said nothing.

"But what about Oxford, Meg?" asked Michelle.

Meg shrugged and started to giggle again. "I've changed my mind. I want to go to Liverpool."

Michelle wondered if Hakim and Anne knew. They'd both been ecstatic when Meg got an offer to study Spanish and French at Trinity College, Oxford, especially Hakim. Michelle had no doubt that Nathan would be in the firing line when they found out Meg had chosen Liverpool instead.

The rest of the meal passed pleasantly enough.

When they asked for the bill, Nathan announced that he and Meg were heading off to a party in Whalley Range.

Michelle paid up and they all stepped outside into the balmy evening. They walked through the graveyard past Chorlton Green where people were sprawled across the grass, drinking from cans and bottles, and enjoying the last few rays of evening sun. After the warm day, dark clouds were gathering, and thunder was predicted later. Meg and Billy strolled on ahead, chatting and laughing, and Michelle hung back with Nathan.

"Billy's not that bad after all, is he?" she said.

Nathan shrugged. "If he makes you happy."

"He makes me very happy. So perhaps you could be a bit nicer to him when he comes round?"

He shrugged again. "Whatever."

"Look after Meg tonight," she whispered, when the four of them parted a few minutes later. She gave him a knowing look. "She didn't seem herself earlier."

Billy took her arm and they crossed over the road and headed to his place. Michelle was wrapped in warm contentment. Will was on a sleepover, they had the house to themselves and she wasn't in work tomorrow

"I thought that went OK, didn't you?" she said, leaning into him.

He laughed and shook his head. "Meg was off her trolley. She was completely stoned."

"I know." Michelle smiled. "I wondered why she was behaving so strangely at first. All that giggling and fixation with the dog. It was only as we were leaving that the penny dropped. I told Nathan to look after her."

"She was well gone."

"Little Meg off her trolley on weed. Whoever would have thought it?" Michelle shook her head. "Fuck me!"

"OK, you're on." Laughing, he grabbed her, and kissed her hard on the mouth. Quickening their pace, they hurried back to his.

Anne

Anne had lain awake for most of the night listening to the violence of the storm. Thunderclaps, initially distant, became deafening. Rain, first a patter, became a roar. Dogs barked wildly and a howling wind slammed tree branches against the window panes. Now, as dawn broke, calm had returned. A chorus of chaffinches sang cautiously in the garden, rainwater dripped rhythmically from gutters, and car tires swished through puddles out on the road.

She sat up and looked over at Meg, the blow-up bed deflating beneath her. Spikes of her blue-and-black hair lay on her pillow like a crown of thorns, and blotches of kohl stained her lily-white face. She was frowning in her sleep.

Anne had watched over Meg all night, the way she used to when she was a new-born, monitoring the rise and fall of her shoulders, listening for her breathing, and watching every movement of her limbs. She would be eighteen next week, a fully-fledged adult. Would the watching over her ever end? Anne recalled the horror of the previous evening, and a slither of fear ran through her. Meg had been the sweetest, most compliant child. She would give anything to have that little girl back again.

Slipping gingerly off the bed, she pulled on her dressing gown, tiptoed out of Meg's room, and went downstairs. She made herself a strong coffee, took it into the living room, and curled up on the battered leather sofa facing the window.

Brantingham Road was Sunday morning quiet. The ground glistened from last night's torrential rain and the orange-tinted sky was pregnant with dark purple clouds. A gust of wind blew through the branches of the cherry blossom in the garden. The empty street and the sight of scattered petals transported her back to the days following her father's death. Unable to sleep, she would stare out of her bedroom window at the yellow-and-black security tape on the street below and watch the flowers from the wilting wreathes cartwheel down the pavement in the breeze.

Her father had been on her mind a lot recently. He'd been a gentle, loving father, but he also possessed a stubborn streak. His bloody-mindedness often made domestic life unpredictable and difficult. If he didn't want to do something, he would flatly refuse without explanation, like a large rock blocking their path and obstructing their plans. Social events were often called off at the last minute, and once an entire holiday to Cornwall was cancelled without any reason given. It wasn't until recently that she realised his anxiety and depression had probably been the cause of this unpredictable behaviour.

And now Meg was exhibiting a similar will of steel. The lady was not for turning, especially when it came to her relationship with Nathan. Hakim had done everything in his power to stop her seeing him, but Meg dug her heels in.

"That boy is trouble," Hakim insisted. "And he's a racist."

"You know nothing about him," she retaliated. "How can he be a racist if he's with me? He's loving and he's kind."

"Loving, kind boys don't have their photos taken with far-right extremists."

"That was ages ago when he was a kid! You're just a patriarch who wants me to stay at home cooking chicken korma and get married to a nice boy from Pakistan."

Hakim's nostrils began to twitch, something that often happened when he was angry. "I want nothing of the kind. I just don't want you dating a racist and a narcissist. Nathan Grainger is just like his father. I will never condone the relationship. *Ever.*"

Daily arguments ensued, followed by weeks of not speaking. Then, when Meg started staying over at Nathan's at the weekends, Hakim walked around the house looking like he'd been badly beaten around the head with a large stick.

Anne stroked his cheek and tried to console him "She's seventeen years old, darling," she said. "I think we have to accept that they're sleeping together. Just think of the positives. At least she's not getting trashed every night in Chorlton Park with God knows who and wandering home on her own. At least we know she's safe if she's with Nathan."

She could not have been more wrong.

Meg had left the house yesterday afternoon with her overnight bag stuffed with revision guides and her laptop. She said that she was going for a meal to celebrate Nathan's birthday with Billy and Michelle, then she and Nathan were going back to his to study for their final exams the following week.

Anne and Hakim had a nice relaxing evening. She'd made gin fizz cocktails, Hakim had cooked a green Thai curry and a yummy lemon sorbet and they'd watched some standup on BBC iplayer. Feeling full and slightly merry, they'd gone to bed around midnight and had sex.

Then, shortly after one, Anne was woken by the doorbell. Feeling a dropping sensation in her stomach, she shook Hakim awake then ran downstairs in her PJs. She opened the front door to see Alex and Meg standing on the doorstep. They were both completely drenched, and Meg was deathly pale. Her make-up was streaked down her face, and her hair and dress were splattered with vomit. She had a vacant expression on her face and looked like a sickly Victorian child ready to drop.

Hakim thundered down the stairs behind her.

"*For God's sake!*" he said, catching hold of Meg as she stumbled over the doorstep. He picked her up, carried her into the living room, and laid her on the sofa.

Anne followed, leaving Alex hovering in the hallway, looking terrified.

Meg had come home drunk numerous times, but never in a state like this.

Anne sat on the sofa. She asked Meg if she was OK, noting her dilated pupils. Meg didn't respond. Instead, she sat upright, her eyes darting around the room.

Hakim hovered over her and shouted, "*Meg, are you OK?*"

Startled, she put her hands over her ears and curled up in a ball, like he'd yelled at a hundred decibels. Then, she scanned the room and grabbed Anne's arm. "Tell them all to go away, Mummy," she said, her words slurred.

"Tell who to go away?"

"Please," she begged.

"Who? Alex and Daddy?"

Hakim stepped towards Alex who was now standing in the doorway. "What's she taken?" he growled.

Shifting from one foot to the other, Alex looked down at the floor without replying.

Hakim raised his voice and repeated, "*What's she taken?*"

"Ket."

"Dear God."

Open-mouthed, Anne looked from Alex to Hakim then back again. "What the hell is Ket?"

"Ketamine," Hakim said. "It's a horse tranquilizer."

Anne froze and looked at Meg, who was now holding out her hands in front of her and moving her fingers slowly in a crab-like motion.

Hakim stepped nearer to Alex. "How long has she been like this?" he asked.

Alex shrugged. "Maybe two or three hours."

"*Three hours!*" Hakim shouted, and Meg curled up into the sofa with her hands over her face, like she was under attack.

"You need to calm down, Hakim," hissed Anne. "You're not helping the situation."

She got up off the sofa, pushed past him and drew Alex into the hall. "Alex, we know you don't want to tell tales on anyone, but we need you to tell us exactly what happened. For Meg's sake."

Alex brushed his long hair away from his face. "Me, Nathan, and Meg ended up at the same party in Whalley Range. Meg and Nathan were having an argument. I think they'd been smoking pot beforehand. A group of them took some Ket. Apparently it usually lasts thirty minutes or an hour max, but Meg wasn't coming down like the rest of them. She was paranoid and saying all kinds of crazy things."

Anne swallowed. "What kind of things?"

Alex looked at the floor. "That she wanted to die."

Anne felt her legs weaken, then she steadied herself against the wall. "Go on."

"I wanted to get an ambulance, but the others said not to. In the end, I managed to get her into a taxi."

"And where was Nathan when all this was going on?" asked Hakim.

"He left."

"*He left,*" Hakim repeated.

Anne could see the white of his knuckles as he gripped the door frame.

She hurried into the kitchen and fetched her purse.

"For the taxi," she said, thrusting a ten-pound note at Alex.

He shook his head, but she pressed it into his palm. "Take it. I'd give you a lift home but ..."

They both looked into the living room at Meg, who was now sitting up straight and moving her head from side to side in slow motion, like she was watching a tennis match.

"Thank you so much for bringing her home and for looking out for her," she said, hugging him, "But please, promise me you won't mention this to anyone."

He shook his head. "I won't."

She practically pushed him out of the front door into the rain. She felt bad, but she simply couldn't bear anyone else to witness her family falling apart.

She slumped back against the door. This was partly her fault. She'd turned a blind eye when she first found out Meg was smoking pot, and she'd kept it secret from Hakim. She knew now that decision had been more about herself than Meg. After two years of Meg being mentally unwell, Anne longed for her to do 'normal' things like her peers, so she'd let the pot-smoking go. If she'd been stricter, maybe Meg wouldn't have graduated to harder drugs. She stared at Meg through the living-room door and started to panic.

She went back into the room. Hakim was standing in front of the fireplace, looking down at his phone.

"We have to get her to A&E to get checked out," she said.

"No need, I'm reading about it now. Apparently, she just needs to sit it out. Her pulse is a little high, but there's nothing to worry about."

"What the fuck is wrong with you?" Anne lowered her voice and looked around to make sure Meg couldn't hear. "She's hallucinating. She could be having a psychotic episode."

Hakim rolled his eyes. "Here we go, catastrophizing as usual. Lots of people hallucinate when they're on drugs, but they don't end up on the psyche ward."

"Meg is not 'lots of people.' She has mental-health issues. She needs to be checked out."

"She's applying for university," Hakim mumbled. "She doesn't need something like this on her medical records."

Anne's jaw dropped and she stepped backwards. "*What the fuck?* She needs to be checked out."

"There really is no need, darling. Look, she's calmed down now and she's dozing off. That's a good sign. Trust me, she'll be fine."

Hakim was right. Meg was certainly less agitated. She was now lying on her side and her eyelids were starting to droop.

Anne went over and checked her pulse, which was normal. She decided she would wait a while longer.

Sure enough, minutes or so later, Meg was fast asleep and snoring lightly, so Anne reluctantly allowed Hakim carry her upstairs and put her to bed.

She insisted on sleeping in the room with her. What if she woke in the night and started hallucinating again? Or choked on her own vomit? Or had some kind of seizure?

She got the blow-up bed from the linen cupboard, pushing Hakim away when he offered to inflate it.

"This is all about bloody Oxford," she whispered. "You're obsessed with her getting in and you don't want to get her checked out at hospital because you think the university might find out and a drugs episode like this might affect her chances. That would never happen. The university admissions don't have access to student medical records. They would never know."

The bed fully inflated, she yanked the plug from the wall and fixed him with a murderous look.

"*Get out*," she said.

She quickly made up the bed, got undressed and got under the covers. Unable to sleep, she tossed and turned, ruminating on what had happened. How bad would Meg have to have been before Hakim sought help? But, more importantly, why had she listened to him instead of following what her instinct was telling her? She'd put Meg's health at risk. She should have simply called for an ambulance there and then.

Eileen

August. What a feckin' wash-out! Relentless showers, slate-grey skies, and not a slither of sunshine. Rain clung to the three of them like a second skin, and they battled with a fierce wind trying to steal their umbrellas. Despite the weather, Deansgate was busy. Grungy-looking students hovered on street corners and people trickled in and out of the bars and restaurants.

Eileen was in great form. Alex was in a much better place, she was on the lash with Anne and Michelle, and she had some fantastic news to share with them later. It had to be said, the tension between them on the tram on the way in had been as taut as a violin string, but even that couldn't subdue her mood.

They passed a gang of blow-ins, a group of thirty-somethings off the train from one of the surrounding towns, looking for a different, better night out. Eileen homed in on their accents. Mancunian, Lancashire, and Yorkshire all sounded the same when she first arrived here twenty years ago, but now she liked to think she could differentiate between them.

"Where's tha gooin' later?" one of the group said. She guessed Lancashire, because of the 'tha' instead of 'you', and the long o in 'going.' Maybe Wigan or Bolton. Scouse was dead easy to spot. It was a world apart and had more in common with Southside Dublin than any English accent. She noticed that the blow-ins tended to dress up a lot: men with gelled hair, starched stripey shirts, and moccasins with no socks, and the women with spray-on tans, dresses and heels. Nobody bothered with a coat, even on a night like this. The group laughed and hollered as they passed.

God love them. The bad weather couldn't dampen their spirits, any more than it could her own.

Michelle and Anne were barely on speaking terms after Meg and Nathan had split and the ketamine incident. Hakim had paid Nathan a little visit afterwards which hadn't helped matters. Eileen was hoping a few drinks in the evening ahead might smooth things over.

Michelle had booked them into Jamie's Kitchen, an upmarket Italian on King Street. It was a former bank, and a listed building. Many of the bank's original features remained: high ceilings, antique chandeliers, mahogany wall-panels. The original bank teller stations had been transformed into a bar area and there was even a vault downstairs, where you could get locked in at private parties.

When they arrived, the waitress showed them to their table on the second-floor balcony.

"Great choice, Michelle," said Eileen, nervously scanning the prices on the menu.

"Yes. Jolly nice," agreed Anne, with a forced smile.

They ordered cocktails and olives.

Michelle looked fabulous in kitten heels and a royal-blue wraparound dress that showed off her curves.

Eileen leaned over the table, removed the curls from the side of Michelle's face, then pulled a face of mock horror. "Matching earrings as well! Jesus, Michelle, what the hell is going on with you?"

"Bugger off," she replied, waving a hand in the air and laughing.

Michelle had the perfumed glow of a woman in love. Eileen was a tad envious. Nowadays, her relationship with Sergio felt as old and weary as the faded jeans and scuffed boots she'd thrown on before coming out. He still wasn't working, and they still argued about money on a daily basis. Things wouldn't be like that for long, though. What had happened on her recent visit to Mayo was going to change everything.

The cocktails arrived, and Eileen raised her glass. "To our Three Musketeers on their exam success! Straight A's for Meg and Nathan. *Wow!* You must both be so proud."

"And to Alex!" said Anne. "For showing so much resilience after everything he's been through."

"*Here, here!*" said Michelle.

Eileen sipped from her glass, the warm Negroni hitting the back of her throat. Alex had come out with a D and two C's in his exams. He hadn't tried much in his studies for the past two years, nor had he shown any interest in going to university. Initially, she and Sergio had been disappointed, but they'd also been secretly relieved. The thought of all that student debt and having to sub him for three years on her salary alone was a daunting prospect. Right now, their priority was his mental health, which was so much better than a year ago. His PTSD symptoms were on the wane and he was working full-time at Tesco, and part-time in a bar in town, with the aim of saving up to go travelling. He'd also acquired a lovely group of friends. A motley, likeable crew, they'd slowly brought him out of his shell after the bombing in a way she and Sergio never could. Rosie was a chatty Marvel film fanatic, with pink hair, Tabatha an artistic redhead, and non-binary Katie had recently become Kit. Daniel was Eileen's favourite, though. A bouncy drama student with several piercings and a grin that stretched from ear to ear, he said "pet" and "sweetie" a lot, and his laughter lit up a room. He too had been at the Arena on the night of the bombing, and he'd done a remarkable job coaxing Alex out of his anxieties and fears of crowded places.

Eileen stabbed at an olive. "So, when are Meg and Nathan off to Liverpool?" she asked.

"Mid-September for Nathan," said Michelle.

"Same here," sniffed Anne.

The awkward silence that followed was broken by loud clatter of plates in the bar area. Meg's decision to choose Liverpool over Oxford had caused ructions at home. Hakim had been in a rage for weeks about it. According to Michelle, he put the blame squarely at Nathan's feet.

Eileen chose the cheapest pasta dish on the menu, and Michelle and Anne plumped for the asparagus risotto. Michelle ordered Prosecco and she and Anne started knocking it back like it was New Year's Eve. Eileen prayed they weren't splitting the bill three ways.

Anne looked uncomfortable. Eileen felt sorry for her. She'd heard all about the ketamine incident and Hakim's visit from Alex and Michelle. She hadn't heard Anne's version of events at all. From what she could gather, Nathan had behaved appallingly. What kind of gobshite buggers off and leaves his girlfriend in a state like that? God knows what might have happened to Meg if Alex hadn't taken her home from that party.

The evening dragged, weighed down by the tension between Michelle and Anne. The words they exchanged were strained, like fragile glass. One mishandling could shatter the entire evening.

Eileen's mood had plummeted. She decided to tell them about her news about Mayo another time. It didn't feel like the appropriate moment. After they'd finished their mains (her pasta was too salty, but the risotto was a resounding success), Michelle disappeared to the bathroom. Anne immediately pulled her chair close to Eileen. For once, Anne was probably the drunkest of the three of them. Her eyes were glazed and intense and she'd slurred her words a couple of times.

"You were right about Nathan all along, Eileen," she said. "I should have listened to you. He really is a little shit. I always felt sorry for him because of the divorce and, when he saved Meg from the crush at the arena, I thought he was the bee's knees. I was actually happy they'd started going out together. Can you bloody believe it?" Curling her lip in disgust, she gulped from her glass. "I know better now. That boy behaves with total impunity and doesn't give a toss for anyone but himself. The thought that he'll be a doctor one day sends a shiver down my spine. Being a doctor requires ethical standards. As far as I can see that little bastard has none whatsoever."

Eileen was about to agree, but at that moment Michelle appeared at the top of the stairs, and they pulled away from each other.

Michelle sat down, a flicker of annoyance crossing her face, as if she knew exactly what they'd been talking about. Fortunately, tiramisu and brandies arrived soon afterwards, and all further mention of offspring was avoided for the remainder of the meal. Michelle told them about a weekend she and Billy were planning in Italy, and Anne disclosed that her mother had been diagnosed with dementia.

Sozzled and subdued, they left the restaurant. They made their way to the tram stop in the wind and rain, Michelle complaining about her cold legs, vowing never to wear a dress again, and Anne clinging on to Eileen as she was unsteady on her feet.

"I'm plastered," Anne said as they neared Exchange Square. "If I don't drink some water soon, I may very well chunder in my handbag."

They hurried into The Printworks leisure complex. Anne staggered to the kiosk nearby to buy a bottle of water and Eileen and Michelle waited for her outside Waxy O'Connor's pub.

Waxy's was one of Manchester's most popular Irish venues. Inside, a live band were singing the Wolfe Tones' "Celtic Symphony", and the raucous crowd was joining in. Buoyed by her recent weekend in Ireland, Eileen had a sudden urge to be in there in the thick of the crowd, surrounded by road signs to Mayo and Dublin, and posters advertising Guinness and Magners. She probably wouldn't even have objected if someone stuck an oversized leprechaun hat on her head. By the time Anne arrived back, she and Michelle were swaying from side to side, singing along.

"One for the road, girls?" Michelle looked at them both expectantly.

Eileen gave her a thumbs-up, then they both looked at Anne who was gulping down her water.

Screwing the top tightly on the bottle, Anne glared at Michelle. "Really? You want me to sit in there like a bloody lemon, while you sing IRA songs?" She pointed in the direction of the Arndale Shopping Centre. "Or have you forgotten how your little chums planted a two-hundred-pound bomb a few hundred yards from here, not that long ago?"

Then, to their amazement, her eyes suddenly filled with tears, and she turned and walked away down the busy street.

Michelle turned to Eileen open-mouthed. "What the hell?"

"Don't mind her. She's bladdered."

The desire for one more drink diminished, they headed to the tram stop, looking around for Anne who was nowhere to be seen.

On the platform, Michelle shook her head in disbelief. "My 'little chums in the IRA'? What was that all about?"

Eileen put her arm around Michelle's shoulders and sighed. So much for her plan to have a few drinks and mend the rift between them.

CHAPTER 9

Michelle

Michelle stepped towards the hall mirror, turned her lanyard the right way around, and inspected the burgundy half-moons under her eyes. God, she hated working nights. Slogging through with a skeleton staff, no cardiologists or neurologists around to consult if you were unsure of anything, and no juniors to do the small jobs, like taking bloods. It felt like battlefield medicine. All she could think of was making it through until morning. Sometimes, in the middle of a particularly tough shift, a voice inside her called out to Nathan not to study medicine. The NHS was already on its knees. What was it going to be like in another six or seven years when he qualified?

Michelle had been genuinely astounded on results day when he'd burst through the door and thrust his results slip at her. Two A stars and one A. How on earth had he done that? As far as she could see, he'd only knuckled down to any serious revision a few weeks before the exams.

"Well done!" she'd said as they exchanged an awkward hug.

He'd pulled away, looked at her coyly and said, "I decided I wanted to be a doctor when I saw you at the hospital the night of the bombing."

"Really?"

"You were awesome, Mum."

Before either of them could say anything else, he charged upstairs to get ready to celebrate with his friends. She watched him go, an involuntary grin spreading over her face. She tried to picture him on a ward round in scrubs, the sheer absurdity of the image making her laugh out loud.

She recalled her own A Level results day: Mum standing by the kitchen sink at a loss for words, Dad coming in from work in his overalls, picking her up, swirling her round the room, and saying, "A wee doctor in the family, no less!" She thought the pair of them would never stop smiling. Three years later, cancer had snatched them both away. First Mum, then Dad. It broke her heart to think that neither of them had lived long enough to see her graduate.

She picked up her car keys and glanced down at the old school photo of Nathan on the hall table. He must have been six or seven when it was taken. How the photographer had got him to sit still long enough to take it, she'd never know. With his crooked tie, white-blonde hair, and two missing teeth, he was a picture of impish innocence. The glass of the frame was cracked, smashed to the floor the day Hakim had come round, a day she wouldn't forget in a hurry.

Hakim had been a good friend for over eighteen years. Michelle had always considered him a gentle, sweet-natured man, but that day she saw a very different side to him. She'd just got in the door from her shift when she heard banging on the front door. When she opened it, Hakim was standing in the porch with a face like thunder, his nostrils flaring.

"I need to see Nathan," he said.

"Hi, Hakim," she said. "Why don't you come in?" She opened the door wide, her stomach quivering. What the hell had Nathan done now?

Hakim shook his head. "No, thanks, Michelle. If you could just get Nathan, please."

"What's it about?"

He clenched his jaw and looked down at his feet. "Nathan gave Meg ketamine at a party last night. She got very unwell and then he abandoned her."

"*What?*" Michelle stepped back, her heart pounding. "Is she OK?" Kids were sometimes brought into work after overdosing on Ket. Going into a K-hole, they called it. It was pretty disturbing.

"She is now. No thanks to Nathan. Fortunately, Alex was there to look after her and bring her home."

Glowering at her, Hakim launched into a diatribe about Nathan, accusing him of all sorts of things and calling him ugly names. She listened, gobsmacked. Hakim had known Nathan since he was a boy. It hurt to think he harboured so much hatred for him.

A few minutes in, Nathan thundered down the stairs behind her. He was in his boxers, and a random blonde trailed behind him, wearing one of his T-shirts and very little else.

Engulfed by a wave of shame, Michelle didn't know where to look.

Hakim pushed past her and headed for Nathan. He was a small man, but his rage was big, and he was strong enough to grab hold of Nathan and drag him across the hallway. He pinned him against the wall, knocking everything off the hall table, including the school photo. The blonde squealed as Hakim's hands went for Nathan's throat.

Michelle was distraught and pleaded with Hakim to stop, but Nathan was calm.

"*I'm still seventeen,*" he croaked. "*Carry on and I'll report you for assaulting a minor.*" He glanced at Michelle then the blonde. "*I've got two witnesses.*"

Pausing for a moment, Hakim let him go. Then, fighting back tears of rage, he left.

Michelle could barely look at Nathan in the days that followed. Meg was fragile and vulnerable, and he was supposed to be her boyfriend. How could he have treated her like that? Had she not brought him up to respect women? There were times recently when she'd felt ashamed to be his mother. Some of the things

Hakim had said about him buzzed in the back of her mind, like annoying wasps she'd couldn't get rid of.

"*What kind of monster gives their girlfriend drugs then buggers off when she's having a bad trip?*"

"*He's a racist, just like his father.*"

"*You need to know your blue-eyed boy is a drug-dealer. Ask him where he gets all his money from. Go on!*"

She wondered if there was any truth in what Hakim said about Nathan dealing drugs. She'd been asking herself where he was getting his money for ages.

The next day, when she was giving Nathan a lift into town, she asked him outright.

"Is it true what Hakim said about you and drugs?" she said. "Are you dealing?"

Nathan leaned his head against the car window. "Yes," he replied. "I've got a stash in my bag to take over to Burnley later on."

She glanced at him, then cursed as the car swerved to the side. "I'm serious, Nathan."

"Of course I'm not dealing fucking drugs!"

"Then where are you getting all your money from? You're out all the time, you buy all those takeaways, yet you've never had a job."

He scrawled a question mark on the misty window with his forefinger. "You have absolutely no faith in me whatsoever, do you, Mummy dearest? You always believe the worst. And now you think I'm the fucking Pablo Escobar of Chorlton."

"I just want the truth."

He turned to her. "Well, here's the truth. It was Meg who got the Ket that night. Your precious little Meg, who is into every drug going. Far more than I am. That's why we split up. I couldn't keep up with her. But nobody will ever believe that because I'm always the bad guy. I admit I was wrong to leave her at the party like that, but she was out of control. I lost it with her. "

"That doesn't answer my question about the money."

He exhaled loudly. "If you must know, Dad made money on some tech shares a while ago, and he doubled my allowance. You were always banging on at me to get a job, but he said I should concentrate on my studies instead. He told me not to tell you. Ask him if you don't believe me."

Still not convinced, she texted Rob later that day. He replied a few hours later with screenshots of bank transfers that confirmed Nathan's story, along with a message.

"I admit giving the boy more cash. Wanted him to spend his time studying for his exams, not pot-washing or shelf-stacking. Let's hope it pays off and he passes his exams."

She'd felt so guilty. Nathan was right about her always believing the worst of him. She'd pictured him in a black hoodie, frequenting crack dens in Salford High Rises and handing small plastic bags to thirteen-year-olds in school uniform in Chorlton Park. She was disgusted with herself. What kind of mother was she to believe that of her only child?

Michelle put the photo back on the hall table. She'd considered discussing Nathan's behaviour towards Meg at the party with Hakim and Anne. She even thought about telling them where he was getting his money, but in the end she let it go. She didn't want any more conflict and she certainly didn't want to tell tales on Meg and her drug habits. Meg was eighteen and old enough to make her own choices. Nathan and Meg had split up shortly afterwards too and everyone had moved on, so there didn't seem much point.

Grabbing her bag and coat, she went out to her car. As she opened the door, her phone pinged in her pocket. It was a text from Eileen with a selfie attached, taken at the restaurant in town the previous week.

Underneath she had written: **"You and Anne look like you've got pokers up your backsides."**

Michelle smiled. It was true. They both looked extremely uncomfortable. Neither she nor Eileen had heard a peep from Anne since her outburst outside Waxy O'Connor's. Michelle was still perplexed and hurt by it all. She'd been floored by Anne's comment – "Your little chums planted a two-hundred-pound bomb nearby".

Growing up in England in the 70's and 80's with parents from Belfast hadn't been easy. Their northern Irish accents attracted attention like the glare of a lighthouse on a dark night. They weren't the southern Irish accents people were used to hearing around the streets of Manchester. To English ears, her loving mum and gentle dad sounded like the voice of the enemy, like

McGuinness or Adams, and the other "Fenian bastards" they heard on the news.

Then there was everything that happened with Uncle Jimmy. It all made her want to cast off her Irishness, like a coat she hated but her parents insisted she carried on wearing. When she was a girl, she quickly learned to keep her head down and her family's republican views at arm's length.

Michelle had confided in very few people about what had happened to Uncle Jimmy. Rob was one and so was Eileen. Michelle had always trusted Eileen implicitly. Yet the more she thought about what Anne had said that night outside Waxy's, the more she couldn't shake off the idea that Eileen had revealed her secret. The betrayal cut deep. Michelle had buried the trauma in a forgotten pond in the farthest reaches of her mind. She never ever wanted to plunge into those murky depths again.

CHAPTER 10

Anne

Meg hopped out of the taxi and ran up the steps of the house. Anne paid the cabbie, almost colliding with a jogger as she stepped onto the pavement with her suitcase. The woman, in glamorous sportswear, spat out something in Russian, then jogged on, her Bichon Frisé trotting behind her. On the other side of the road, a man in a Kalmar chemise was running along the pavement on his phone, his loose white trousers flapping in the breeze. Anne remembered how everyone in London was always in such a frantic rush, even at nine thirty on a Saturday morning.

Meg pressed the buzzer for the second time and handed Anne the bouquet of roses that had been propped by the door. Anne read the card attached.

Forty years may have passed but the memories of our dear friend and neighbour Colonel Harry McFarland have never faded.

Much love to you all – Eleanor, Anne and Hannah

William and June Fletcher xx

Anne glanced over the road at Number 13. She thought she saw a curtain move. Darling William and June. They must both be well into their eighties by now. Meg rang the buzzer for a third time and tutted impatiently.

Anne stepped back and looked up at the window of the flat on the first floor. Whenever she tried to remember what the three-storey Georgian townhouse looked like before the conversion into flats, only fleeting images came to her, never the house in its entirety. She could recall the wide staircase and dark-oak banister she and Hannah used to slide down, her father's musty office lined with books and army memorabilia. Then there was the kitchen and the vivid green Mary Quant wallpaper she and Hannah persuaded their mother to buy, and Slinky's tartan cat bed nestled in the corner of her bedroom. Her parents rarely entertained, but one New Year's Eve there had been a fondue party. Her mother had looked amazing in a burgundy-velvet maxi dress and a black choker, her father had worn a dicky bow, and they'd danced very badly to The Stones' "Honky Tonk Women" under the chandelier in the dining room.

Nowadays, the three flats were occupied by Hamish, a quietly spoken violinist from the Scottish Highlands who lived on the ground floor, her mother on the first and, after her divorce from Peter, Hannah and her daughter Bea had moved into the attic flat. Hannah didn't pay any rent, but then she had her mother living below her – something Anne would have paid thousands of pounds to avoid.

After what seemed like an age, they were buzzed in, and they hurried up the stairs. When her mother finally opened the door, Anne was taken aback.

In her youth, she had been a beauty in the mould of Grace Kelly. As she'd aged, she'd remained slim and elegant in pastel shades and cashmere. There'd been weekly trips to the hairdresser to keep her hair ash-blonde and well-trimmed, and she constantly criticised other women for "letting themselves go". Now, under a stained pink dressing gown, she looked shrunken and bony. Her skin was papery and jaundiced, and her hair snowy-white, wispy and unkempt. Suddenly Anne felt a pang of pity for her – something she rarely felt.

"Hi, Granny!" Meg kissed her cheek, then ran past her down the hallway and into the spare room. Today she was dressed in full emo glory: blue hair, nose-ring, fishnets, and olive-green twelve-hole Doc Martens.

"Good God," said her grandmother, staring after her, "She looks like a common prostitute."

Anne bit her lip, the pity she'd felt a few moments before fading quickly.

She followed her mother's slow shuffle down the hallway. It had been six months since her last visit, and if it wasn't for her father's anniversary, she'd probably have left it for another six. She was already dreading the thought of the memorial dinner that evening at his old military club on the Common. The average age would be a hundred and two, and none of them would remember who she was. Some wouldn't have a clue who her father was either. Anne had decided she was going to try and wriggle out of it. She and Meg would pay a quiet visit to the grave tomorrow instead.

Not long after their arrival, Bea burst through the door, looking for Meg. Though the cousins didn't see each other often, they were in constant touch on social media. Sixteen approaching twenty-five, Bea was dressed in flesh-coloured designer leggings, a skin-tight crop-top, and fake tan smeared ad-hock over her face. The poor girl had inherited her father Pete's large horsey features and none of Hannah's prettiness, but she was an absolute hoot. She had recently replaced her upper-class accent with an estuary English one that she hadn't quite mastered. The result was hilarious. Anne wondered how it had gone down at her all-girl's private school in Carshalton.

The girls disappeared into Meg's room then headed off to Camden Market soon afterwards, Meg delighted with the hundred pounds her granny and Hannah had given her for passing her A Levels. Anne had warned her sister and mother in advance not to talk about universities or mention the word Oxford if they wanted a pleasant weekend. Anne had heard enough about that to last a lifetime.

On results day, Meg had sat her and Hakim down at the kitchen table and announced that she was declining the offer from Trinity in Oxford and going to Liverpool instead.

Hakim stared at her in disbelief. "This is to do with Nathan Grainger, isn't it? You're seeing him again."

Meg rolled her eyes. "No, I'm not. All of that is over and I've moved on. I've tried to talk to you about this before, Daddy, but you simply wouldn't listen. The reason I don't want to go to Oxford is because I'm not sure I'll be able to cope with the pressure."

Hakim scraped his chair back and stood up. "You'll be absolutely fine. We've already looked into it and they've got lots of support in place at Trinity. There are mental health hotlines and counsellors on hand at all hours."

Meg slapped her palm on the table and raised her voice. "Daddy, you're not listening. I never told you, but after my interview at Trinity I talked to some of the students in the canteen. They said a lot of students there, particularly the international ones, study from seven in the morning until seven at night." She shook her head. "If I spend the next three years in a competitive atmosphere like that, I'll have a nervous breakdown. I know I will."

Hakim stood up and leant back on the worktop with his arms folded. "But you're giving up a chance of a lifetime, Meg. Having a degree from Oxford opens so many doors. People like us rarely get offered an opportunity like this."

"People like us?" Meg scrutinised his face. "You mean people with brown faces? Well, I'm very sorry to disappoint you, Daddy, but I'm not going to risk my mental health just so the University of Oxford can tick its diversity boxes."

"That's not what I'm saying. I'm simply saying you should value your achievement – and not throw it away! " He paused. "Maybe you just need a bit more time to think about it."

Meg stood up. "No, I don't. I've made up my mind. I'm going to Liverpool. *End of.*"

Hakim was about to launch into a tirade when Anne held her palm in the air. She'd been listening carefully to every word Meg had said.

"That's enough, Hakim," she said calmly. "It's Meg's decision and Meg's future. If she wants to go to Liverpool, she goes to Liverpool."

So, Liverpool it was.

Anne had initially been delighted and surprised when Meg had been offered the place at Trinity. Despite being a high achiever at school, she had always been considered less intelligent than her sisters and none of them had been considered for Oxbridge. Anne was convinced her natural talent for languages got her the place. She seemed to soak them up like a sponge. Hakim was right: a degree from Oxford certainly did open doors. Anne had seen that with her peers at her private school, St. Joan's. Those who'd gone on to Oxbridge had slipped easily into jobs in finance and law and media after graduating. She couldn't deny that she been a tad disappointed when Meg decided not to go. Yet part of her had been secretly relieved. She had her own concerns about Meg living a four-hour drive away. What if she became unwell again, or went overboard with the partying and the drugs? Liverpool, on the other hand, was on their doorstep and Meg knew at least three other kids who were going.

The more she thought about it, the more Anne realised Meg had made the right decision. Not so Hakim. He traipsed around the house for weeks like a sick puppy. Sometimes, she wondered if he'd ever really understood anything about Meg's mental-health issues at all. Major life-changing events, like going away to university, were stressful and anxiety-inducing and needed careful thought.

After Bea and Meg left, Anne wandered down to the shops by the tube station. It was midday and London was at full throttle. As a girl, she'd always hated the noise of the big city: the buzz of motorbikes, buses forever stopping and starting, sirens howling day and night, and the rattle of overland trains. It all made her want to put her hands over her ears and scream. She felt exactly the same about London now. The hustle and bustle, as well as the grating presence of her mother, meant she never wanted to stay for more than two days at a time.

Growing up, there'd been a fish-and-chip shop, a small flower stall, and a newsstand on the road by the Tube station. Now, there was a deli, a Boots, a Spanish tapas place, a Lebanese restaurant, three fast-food outlets, and a florist that did a side-line in expensive trinkets. She stopped at the deli to buy something for lunch, then headed into the florist's. Baulking at the price-tag, she reluctantly handed over thirty-two pounds for a bunch of lilies to put on her father's grave.

On her way back, she stopped by the newsstand outside the Tube. Forty years ago tomorrow, she and Hannah had walked past that very spot with her Aunt Lizzie after she'd been dispatched to fetch them from school. On the billboard, written in bold letters was the horror of what those animals had done to their father. Lizzie had quickly dragged them away in an attempt to stop them reading, but it was too late. Anne hadn't fully processed what Lizzie had told them back at the school. When she saw it printed in black-and-white, she still didn't believe it.

As she made her way back to the flat the memory made her feel out of sorts. She ached with sadness for the traumatised fourteen-year-old she was at the time.

Later, Anne and her mother sat in the kitchen drinking Chablis and eating quiche and salad. The flat was crammed with antique furniture from the house before it was converted into flats. The oak dressers and wardrobes were far too big for the small rooms and blocked out the little light that slipped through the small windows, making the rooms dark and oppressive. Old photos and a collection of Hogarth prints dotted the walls. There was only one picture of her father when he was in his twenties. He looked terribly dashing in his army uniform.

Anne topped up her mother's glass. "I think it's probably better if Meg and I don't come to the dinner tonight," she said. "The way she dresses is a little inappropriate."

"Or rather the way she undresses."

"Exactly. She may very well trigger a number of strokes or heart attacks. Bea isn't going either. I'd rather not leave them alone. Lord knows what they'd get up to."

"Whatever has happened to Megan? Is she on drugs?"

"Of course not." Anne topped up her own glass. Never one for daytime drinking, her mother's presence drove her to it. "She's a teenager. It's just a phase she's going through."

"You were never like that."

Oh yes, I was. I was up to lots of things at that age. You just never noticed.

Her mother sipped her wine. "I found her pills."

"Sorry?"

"Megan's anti-depressants. I saw them in her toiletry bag in the bathroom." She put her fork down and sighed. "So she takes after your father, then."

Anne clenched the stem of her wine glass. Whilst most grandparents might inquire about their granddaughter's mental health in the form of a tentative question, her mother dealt it as a cruel blow.

Anne cleared her throat. "Meg hasn't had it easy these past few years. She found secondary school extremely tough, then there was the bombing. She takes the anti-depressants to help with her anxiety. Lots of kids take them these days."

A silence followed and they both listened to the grandfather clock in the hallway. Its ticking could be heard in every room.

Her mother sighed. "Your father had anxiety as well as depression, but it didn't have a name back then. He'd shake like a leaf whenever he had to do any kind of public speaking, and he'd always drink two or three stiff whiskies beforehand."

"I never knew that."

"He used to send me to the doc's for a prescription for Valium, then take them himself."

"Really? Poor Daddy."

"Poor me. I had to put up with it all."

Anne gave her a tight-lipped smile. "Meg is getting lots of help. She'll be fine."

"I do hope so. I'd never wish that illness on anyone. It ruined your father's life. And mine." She put her hand to her forehead. "Oh, dear. It all ended so badly, didn't it? I wish I'd done more."

Anne squirmed in her seat, shocked to see tears in her mother's eyes. She was witnessing a rare chink of emotion in her armour, and she hadn't a clue how to react.

"What on earth could you have done, Mummy?" she said. "It wasn't your fault he was murdered."

"I think the wine's making me squiffy." She sat up straight, composing herself. "How about a nice cup of tea?"

To make up for not attending the dinner, Anne spent a lot of time that evening getting her mother ready. She blow-dried her hair, made her face up to look less corpse-like, and dressed her in turquoise silk with a royal-blue pashmina.

"Sorry we can't make it," she said, as Hannah took her mother's arm and ushered her towards the stairs.

"Why break a habit of a lifetime, Anne?" she replied, with a frosty smile.

When they'd gone, Anne made herself a stiff gin and tonic. As she was cutting some lemon, she got a text from Eileen inviting her for coffee the following week. She felt herself redden. She'd been completely rat-arsed the last time she saw Eileen and Michelle when they'd gone to the restaurant in town. She could hardly remember anything she did or said after leaving, except hauling herself into a taxi to get home. She'd stayed in bed the next day with the most brutal hangover.

Armed with her Kindle, and her gin, she made her way downstairs, then through the communal door that led into the back garden. It was a pleasant autumn night and a bright moon hung in the clear sky, like an oversized coin. She sat on the bench at the end of the narrow lawn. Rickety and splintered now, it had been there since she was a girl. Her father would sit on it on summer evenings, sometimes with a book or a newspaper, always with a cigarette. In the days after his death, she'd spent hours on it, curled up in a ball, trying to escape the madness going on inside the house.

She sipped her gin, opened her Kindle and started reading her novel, a love story about a young Scottish woman who joins the French resistance in the Second World War in order to find her missing lover, a British airman. Anne's father had been stationed in France for part of the war and, as she'd been reading, he'd kept coming to mind.

Tonight she was finding it hard to concentrate. Her thoughts kept wandering back to what her mother had said earlier at lunch about him suffering from anxiety. It brought a lump to her throat. How hard it must have been, a man in his position in the military, in an era when mental health issues were a taboo. His was a world of macho behaviour and control, and the slightest hint of frail mental health or fear would have been seen as weakness. Keeping up the pretence must have been exhausting. Was it any wonder he spent entire days in bed?

She recalled what her mother had said about Meg inheriting his darkness. Her putting it into words had sent a shiver of fear through Anne. It was something that was always present in her mind, like a crow on her shoulder, its claws digging into her skin. Yet Anne clung to the hope that Meg's struggles were a passing phase, a teenage thing she would grow out of. She'd got help early on. Everyone said early intervention made a huge difference. She prayed that was the case.

Not long afterwards she heard Meg and Bea's laughter at the front of the house. She shouted out to them to come and join her. They burst through the communal door. Flush-faced and giggling, they sauntered across the lawn and sat down on either side of her on the bench. Meg nuzzled into the crook of her neck, and Bea put her head on her left shoulder. They both reeked of weed. Anne couldn't help smiling and wondering what her father would have made of his bad-ass granddaughters.

CHAPTER 11

Eileen

Sinéad Foley held out two tickets for a céilí the following Saturday at St. Kentigern's Irish Club. "All the proceeds go to Syrian refugees arriving in County Mayo next month," she said. She looked at Eileen expectantly.

"That's a shame." Eileen crossed her fingers behind her back. "We're away that weekend."

She was on her way to meet Michelle for coffee, when she'd been kettled in by Sinéad and her friend Carmel Doherty outside the library. Eileen had only met Carmel a few times, but Sinéad had once recounted her life story in such minute detail that it now felt like Carmel was an old friend. Apparently, Carmel had grown up in a rundown old semi on the same road as Anne. Her late mother, a Mayo woman, had severe mental-health issues, and Carmel had recently discovered that years ago she had given birth to a baby in one of the notorious Mother and Baby homes in Ireland that were all over the news, and forced to give her baby away. Carmel had now embarked on a search for her sibling.

"You couldn't make it up," Sinéad had gushed. "It's like something out of a book."

Sinéad lived four doors down from Eileen on the estate. Her parents were Kerry people, and she was a governor at St. Joseph's, the local Catholic primary. Her daughter Ciara was an Irish dancing champion and, before it was sold to make way for flats, Sinéad's life had revolved around Chorlton Irish Association Club on High Lane. She organised County Association dances, charity events and was head honcho on the annual St. Patrick's Day parade committee. She'd campaigned for years to keep the club open before it was sold. Bereft, Sinéad was now transferring all her energies to an Irish club in Fallowfield instead.

Eileen liked Sinéad. She was a good woman, with a big heart, but the way she roared about her Irishness and waved her fluorescent tricolour above her head twenty-four-seven was too much. She was forever trying to rope Eileen into Irish-related activities. It made her cross. Why, just because she was Irish, did Sinéad assume she'd want to spend her Saturday nights at a céilí or paint a shamrock on her face on 17th March? On the rare occasions she and Sergio could afford a night out, they went to the San Juan Tapas bar on Beech Road, or Coriander, the Indian, opposite Southern Cemetery. Sometimes, they might push the boat out and go to Home, the arty cinema complex in town, followed by a meal in the restaurant there. Eileen had a Spanish husband, a bilingual son, and her job teaching English as a foreign language at the local college brought her in contact with people of all nationalities and cultures. If anything, she felt European and never more so since Brexit. While she would always be proud to be Irish and longed to return to Ireland, she didn't feel the need to flash her Irish identity badge every minute of the day.

Making her excuses, Eileen hurried off to meet Michelle at Tea Hive, a café near the library. It was a tepid September day, with a slight breeze.

When she arrived, Michelle was sitting at one of the wrought-iron tables outside, engrossed in a copy of the *Guardian*.

Michelle folded the paper and laid it down on the table. **No-deal Brexit Could be as Bad as the 2008 Financial Crash**, said the headline.

Eileen sighed. The whole fecking mess was never-ending, and the Irish border issue was a complete farce. Thankfully, it wasn't something she'd have to worry about for much longer.

She pulled out a chair and sat opposite Michelle. "I've just been accosted by Sinéad Foley trying to sell me tickets for a céili again." She rolled her eyes. "Talk about a Plastic Paddy."

Michelle gave her a sharp look. "That's not very nice."

"What?"

"Calling someone a Plastic Paddy. It's insulting. You'd never refer to someone who was celebrating their Italian or Jamaican heritage as plastic, would you?"

"Get you." Reddening, Eileen picked up the menu and buried her face in it. "Sinéad's so over the top, though," she mumbled.

"Why? She's only observing her heritage. Surely that's a good thing?" Michelle sat back and folded her arms. "I was only thinking about this the other day. In America, if you have Irish ancestry, you call yourself Irish American, but in England, you call yourself

Manchester Irish or Birmingham Irish or London Irish. Nobody would ever call themselves English Irish. You identify with your city, not the country. It's like the term 'English Irish' is too loaded because of the bad history and conflict between the two countries. It's fraught. Almost a contradiction."

"I've never thought about it like that, but I suppose you're right. And Anglo Irish is something different entirely."

"A Protestant on a horse, according to Brendan Behan."

Eileen laughed. "Love it!"

"It was one of my dad's favourite lines."

Eileen put the menu down. "So, do you consider yourself Manchester Irish then?"

"Yes. I suppose I do."

Eileen ordered a latte and a slice of carrot cake, which arrived shortly afterwards. When she started to quiz Michelle about her upcoming weekend away in Verona with Billy, she sensed an aloofness and lack of warmth in her responses. Perplexed, she racked her brains, trying to think if she'd done or said anything to offend her. After a while, she leant over and tapped her on the arm.

"Are we OK?" she asked. "You seem a bit distant."

"Actually, I'm a bit cross with you." Michelle stared at a young mother unloading her baby from her bicycle-seat outside the library then looked back at Eileen. "Did you tell Anne the things I told you about my Uncle Jimmy?"

Eileen swallowed her carrot cake quickly. Coughing, she put her hand over her mouth. "No. Why?"

"That time outside Waxy O'Connor's? The comment she made about my 'IRA chums'?"

Eileen shook her head vehemently. "I swear to God, Michelle, I never told her a thing."

A brief silence followed, then Michelle sighed. "OK. Forget about it."

"I'd never tell anyone about that. I know how strongly you feel about keeping it secret."

Michelle stuck her bottom lip out. "Sorry, pet, I shouldn't have doubted you. It's just that it was such a random thing for her to say, that's all."

"I thought she was having a dig at both of us, to be honest. Her comment had an edge to it. It was completely out of character and a bit weird."

It wasn't long before they were chatting with their usual familiarity and warmth once again, so Eileen decided to bite the bullet.

Pushing her plate to one side, she took a few deep breaths and said, "I have news."

"You're preggers?"

"Nope."

"You've decided to transition and change your name to Éamon?"

Eileen laughed and shook her head. "Not that I know of."

"What then? Spit it out."

"We're moving back to Mayo."

Michelle's face fell with the speed of a broken lift. "What?"

"It was all decided when I was over there the other week."

At the start of August, Eileen's mother had ended up in the County Hospital after a fall. Her father had insisted on paying for Eileen to fly back to Mayo for a few days. When she got to Glencorrib, though, her mother was home and seemed perfectly fine. The next day, she discovered the real reason he had wanted her back.

Ever since their visit the previous summer, he had been full of remorse for his homophobic remarks in front of Shannon about the Mayo goalkeeper, and he was also mortified about the fireworks incident that had triggered Alex's anxiety attack. On their return to Manchester, her parents started ringing Alex every week and sending him money every month. Eileen suspected they were feeling guilty about not giving him the same attention as they gave to Nicky's boys. She'd never blamed them for that, though. How could they not spoil their grandchildren when they lived on their doorstep?

On the evening of her arrival, her father suggested a walk. It had been a soft day. Drizzle hovered in the air, dusk was falling over the lake, and the last rays of evening light tiptoed across the water. There were few cars on the road, and when they were about ten minutes from Glencorrib, he stopped and pointed at a spot on the right.

"That plot belongs to us," he said. "It's yours if you want to build on it." He smiled. "There's also money to help with a house."

"Are you serious?" Eileen was taken aback. She had no idea her parents owned any land at all. "Is this because of what happened with Alex last summer? You don't have to do this, Da."

He smiled again, his big moon-face full of love. "Nothing to do with the fireworks, pet. Your mother and I have been talking about it for a while now. We know how much you want to come home." He winked. "Call it a little bribe."

"But what's Nicky going to say about it?"

"Don't worry about Nicky. She's had her fair share of money from us."

Back at Glencorrib, Eileen did some number-crunching. With the money her father was giving her, plus what they'd get for the sale of the house in Chorlton, they'd have enough to build a decent-sized house. Giddy with excitement, she called Sergio. He was delighted, as she knew he would be. She suspected he'd go to the ends of the earth to escape the rut he was in in Manchester. They only had Alex to persuade now.

Michelle looked at her glumly. "So, you're really going?" Eileen put a hand on her arm. "Not for at least a year. We've got to sell up here and get permission to build first."

"What about jobs?"

"There's ESOL teaching work for me at the local Community College with asylum seekers. The live music scene in Galway city is vibrant, so maybe Sergio will get something in the bars and clubs there."

"And Alex?"

"He loves it there and he's well up for it. Most of his friends are off to uni anyway, and he's determined to go travelling."

Michelle stirred her coffee absently. "I'm happy for you. I really am." She sighed. "It's just a bit of a shock."

"I've wanted to go back for ages, but we could never afford it. To be honest, since Brexit it's never been the same here for me or Sergio. We don't feel welcome. We feel," she said, making quotation marks in the air with her forefingers, "'other'."

"You never said."

"It was never as bad for me as it was for Sergio. His 'otherness' was more evident. I don't know if I ever told you but, in the weeks after the referendum, he and his friends actually stopped speaking in Spanish in public because they got so many dirty looks in the street. Can you imagine that? After living here for twenty years?"

"It's not like that now, though."

"No, but it's something you never forget. Then there was the fiasco of the citizenship papers. Being asked to pay thousands, after being here all these years." She gestured at the waitress to bring over the bill. "Small things like that eat away at you over time, Michelle. We'd built a life and raised our son here, then overnight all the rules changed."

"Sounds like you've made up your mind."

Eileen bit her lip and nodded. "Afraid so, pet."

Michelle looked away, her eyes brimming with tears.

PART FOUR

CHAPTER 12

Fourteen months later

December 2019

Michelle

The odds were looking good for a white Christmas. The back garden was blanketed in an inch of pristine snow and in the distance The Meadows shimmered in a silvery blue light. Snow dusted the lines of tall pines in the depth of the woods, and sunlight filtered through the branches making dappled shadows. The scene reminded Michelle to buy a tree. She and Nathan could get one together tomorrow at the pop-up place in Longford Park.

Rob was sitting on the sofa by the window, his face buried in a copy of the *Daily Mail*. He'd put on even more weight since she'd last seen him and his face was permanently flushed, no doubt the result of stuffing his face with copious amounts of Rioja and chorizo in Marbella's finest restaurants. Michelle hadn't been one bit surprised to learn of his type two diabetes diagnosis. He'd had all the necessary tests in Spain but, of course, in his view foreign doctors weren't to be trusted so he was in Manchester to get a second opinion at a Bupa clinic in town.

Rob had picked Nathan up from his halls of residence in Liverpool that morning and the pair of them were off to see City play Arsenal at the Etihad. She was surprised the match was still going ahead. The motorway was gridlocked because of the snow, and it had taken them over two and a half hours instead of the usual fifty minutes to get back. Nathan was in high spirits, delighted to be going to the match with his dad, like old times. It was the first time she'd seen him since he left in September. He hadn't even been back for the mid-term break. That morning, when he'd walked through the door with Rob, her heart had soared, like a bird after catching a fat fish in water.

She'd been surprised how much she'd missed him. Initially, she thought she'd be revelling in her new-found freedom. No more slamming of the front door at three in the morning, no more scenes of devastation in the kitchen the next morning after a late-night fry-up, and no more picking up his crap from floors all around the house. She was going to get a load of new hobbies, go away for mini-breaks, and finally be able to relax at home with Billy. Well, look how that turned out!

She hated the silent empty house. She missed Nathan's clatter and laughter, the strange noises he made when he was on his Xbox with his friends, and his grime tunes blaring out from the attic. Their brief exchanges in the mornings, as she dashed out to work and he went to college, meant the world to her now. Along with her work, Nathan had been her reason for getting up every morning for the last eighteen years. The day he left for Liverpool, she felt like a chunk of her heart had fallen off. When he returned and threw his bag of dirty washing at her feet earlier, she'd rolled her eyes, but inside she'd felt a pang of joy, the same joy she used to feel when she picked him up on his first days at nursery as he ran to her with his arms open wide. It wouldn't last, of course. In a week's time she'd be ticking off the days on the calendar until term started again.

She placed a mug of tea on the side table next to Rob – milky, two sugars, despite the diabetes. He was busy reading a story about Trump's possible impeachment and barely looked up from his paper.

Michelle perched on a stool at the breakfast bar. "Did Nathan talk much about uni on the drive back?" she asked.

He looked at her over his reading glasses. "Said he was having a whale of a time. Parties galore. And that everyone was very woke."

"Meaning?"

Rob put his paper down and picked up his mug. "Trans rights, LGBT rights, that type of thing. Everyone's rights, unless you're a white male, apparently."

"His words or yours?"

"His." He slurped his tea and grinned. "I think his love life is pretty busy. Apparently med students are very popular with the girls."

Michelle fiddled with a coaster and sighed. "'Twas ever thus. Even the mingers on our course had a small following. Oddly enough, it was never the case for us females."

"True. I don't remember you fighting off many suitors when we met."

"Shame. If I had been, I wouldn't have ended up with you."

"*Touché*. Anyway, how *is* your love life, Michelle? You've been with Billy Boy for a while now. Any sign of him moving in?"

"None of your business," she said, a little too quickly.

Blushing, she picked up her phone and willed Nathan to come downstairs before they had a fully blown row. These days, she and Rob couldn't be in the same room with each other for more than five minutes without going for the jugular. Why couldn't they have a mature, amicable relationship, like other divorced couples she knew?

He picked up his paper again, Michelle stared at her phone, and they waited in an uncomfortable silence.

She clicked on a photo from her weekend in Verona with Billy back in September. They were both sitting outside a pizzeria, draped in late evening sunshine and he had his arm around her. She was flush-faced, looking up at him, smiling. They'd headed off for the city-break the week after Nathan left for Liverpool. Billy had put Will on a train to Glasgow to spend a few days with Bridget, and they'd escaped for four whole days. Giddy and untethered, they'd visited Juliet's supposed house, the Scala family tombs, eaten exquisite food, and spent mornings having great sex in their boutique hotel bedroom. Pure bliss.

Things seemed perfectly normal when they got back but, in November, as the winter days started to chill so did Billy's feelings for her. All the funny texts, spur-of-the-moment visits and lengthy phone calls stopped, and he started to disappear for days on end without telling her where he'd been. When she eventually did speak to him, the warmth in his voice had been replaced by short frosty answers to her questions. She'd always known that she was punching above her weight, and that the day would come when he would leave. Yet she'd never imagined the end would be like this. She'd been gobsmacked when Eileen told her what Sergio had seen that night outside the Spread Eagle in Chorlton. Sergio had only met Billy a couple of times, so Michelle couldn't be a hundred percent sure it was Billy he'd seen and not someone who looked like him. He could easily have been mistaken. Anyway, she'd know the truth by the end of the day. She was going around to Billy's that evening, to confront him.

Rob took off his reading glasses and cleaned them with the arm of his jumper. "Nathan told me your Uncle Jimmy isn't well."

She nodded. "He's on the stroke ward at our place. I'm going in to see him later. It's not looking good."

"Watch out for the queue of visitors."

Flushed with anger, she shook her head.

Rob put his glasses back on and then held up his palms. "Just saying. He's not going to get many visitors after what he did, is he?"

"He's a dying man. Have some respect." Her lip curled in disgust. "You know, Rob, you really are a nasty bastard."

Relieved to hear Nathan bounding downstairs, she hopped off her stool. A few seconds later, he burst into the room wearing his Man City scarf and hat. His puffa jacket enveloped him. He'd lost weight since he'd been away and grown his hair long. She liked it. She thought it made him look kinder, and less preppy.

Rob looked at the kitchen clock. "We need to get going," he said, grabbing his coat and lumbering off the couch.

A few minutes after they left, she found Rob's City scarf down the side of the sofa. She ran outside, waving it in the air and shouting after them, but they'd gone too far down the street to hear her. She watched them walk away, Rob's arm around Nathan's shoulder, snow falling soundlessly around them, the sky silvery blue above their heads.

In the years to come, Michelle would recall that scene but in her mind she would play out a different ending. She'd imagine Rob hearing her shouts and coming back for the scarf. She would tell him to take care and look after himself, they would exchange a little joke, then he would go on his way, thinking that she didn't hate him after all. But none of that happened. Instead, the last thing she'd ever said to him was to call him a nasty bastard.

Anne

Clay Corner was bustling. They'd already turned away three walk-ins that morning and declined another two over the phone. Carla's idea to offer free mince pies and a glass of mulled wine with every booking had brought in a flood of customers. With a week to go before Xmas, they were fully booked every day.

Anne watched Carla quietly singing to herself in Spanish, as she set out paint tubes and palettes for a group coming in any minute to celebrate a fortieth birthday. She'd hit the jackpot when she'd found Carla. Small and wiry, she had a head of black corkscrew curls, and a tattoo of Frieda Kahlo's face on her upper arm. Far more mature than her twenty-three years, she was well-organised, self-motivated, and wonderful with children. Every morning, as she burst through the door like a ray of Mediterranean sunshine, Anne wondered what her parents had done to raise such a positive-thinking, well-balanced young woman.

Anne looked around the busy studio with a satisfied smile. She remembered how she'd almost had to close down in 2016, when she was homeschooling Meg. Things couldn't be more different now. Business was positively booming.

She took some extra brushes and a pot of glitter over to a table of ten-year-old girls by the window. She spotted Meg outside, crossing the road. Hakim had picked her up from Liverpool for the holidays the day before and today she was taking over from Carla, who was having a well-deserved afternoon off to go Christmas shopping.

Snow whirled around Meg as she zigzagged between the slow-moving cars, her yoga mat under her arm. Her legs were spidery, in black leggings and pointy ankle boots, and her top half was burrowed in an oversized black-and-white faux fur. The emo look had long gone, thank God. The nose-rings, white foundation, and blue hair had been replaced by a neat French bob and natural-looking make-up. These days, she had some colour in her cheeks too. Even her granny said she looked well when they'd visited her in the home recently. Not once had she referred to her as "a common prostitute". Anne felt lucky. Michelle hardly ever heard from Nathan, and Alex was thousands of miles away in New York, but Meg came home from uni every other weekend. Maybe that would all stop now she was going out with Josh, but at the moment she was still very much part of their lives.

Meg came through the door, shook the snowdrops from her hair and wiped her boots. Carla left shortly afterwards, then Anne followed Meg into the back room. After unravelling her layers, Meg donned an apron and put her lunch, a tofu salad and a berry smoothie she'd carefully prepared that morning, into the fridge. Noticing they were down to the last few mince pies, Anne grabbed her coat and went out to get some more from Ludo, the French deli a couple of doors down, where they had a daily order.

As she was passing Etchell's newsagent's, she bumped into Michelle coming out. Michelle looked snug in a khaki bubble coat that almost reached her ankles and her curls were squashed under a green bobble hat.

Six months had passed since Nathan and Meg had split up and Hakim had paid Nathan a visit. Anne had been appalled by his violent behaviour yet at the same time she'd felt quite proud – she hadn't thought Hakim had it in him to give anyone a good pasting. The bad feeling generated by the whole sorry episode had kept her and Michelle at arm's length for a while. Then, at a gathering at Eileen's house in October, she and Michelle had got very drunk and made up, agreeing not to let what had happened sully their friendship. Everyone concerned had moved on by then and things had got back on an even keel.

"Can you believe this weather?" Anne said, tightening her coat around her and stepping under the shop awning. "What are you up to?"

Michelle followed her. "Just popped out for a get-well card for my uncle," she said, holding up a white envelope and slipping it into her bag. "He's had a stroke. I'm on my way to see him at the hospital."

"Oh no. Sorry to hear that."

"I haven't seen him in years. The stroke was inevitable, really. He was a raving alcoholic." She pointed over at Clay Corner. "Looks busy in there."

"It is. Meg's back from Liverpool and she's helping me out today. We're giving away mince pies and we've run out so I'm off to get more from Ludo. Did you hear Sergio's working there now?"

Michelle nodded and rubbed her gloved hands together. "Eileen said he's covering maternity leave for someone before the move to Ireland. Apparently he's not a miserable sod any more now he's got a job."

"He's certainly very jolly and chatty when he delivers the mince pies to us in the mornings. Have you heard anything from Eileen in New York?"

"Not a thing. What would I give to be in New York at Christmas! Lucky bitch. Anyway, how's Meg? Is she enjoying Liverpool?"

"Yes. I was convinced she'd be doing some hard-core partying in her first year, but instead she's flung herself into herbal teas and sobriety."

"You're kidding?"

"She's a changed girl, Michelle. She's into healthy eating and daily yoga, and whenever she comes home she stocks up on soya milk, raw honey and organic vegetables at Unicorn, the vegan co-op."

"Bloody hell."

"It's driving Hakim mad. She lectures him about nutritional value and the dangers of processed food. He listens politely, then calmly points out that all the dahls, curries and naan he's been cooking for years haven't contained any processed ingredients either. I thought he was going to have a breakdown when she turned vegan and refused to eat his chicken korma."

Michelle laughed and waved her hand in the air. "I'll eat her share. Please give me Hakim's chicken korma!"

"I tell him to think about the days when she was getting rat-arsed and high every night in Chorlton Park. Quinoa and tofu are such a small price to pay. At least we know what she's up to if she's in the vegan co-op."

"True. I've noticed that university students aren't as wild as they were in our day, though, Anne. Apart from Nathan, of course. I read recently that a lot of generation Z kids are turning away from drink and drugs."

Anne nodded. "Meg's new boyfriend Josh is a clean-living type too."

"Yes?" Michelle raised a quizzical eyebrow.

"We met him briefly when we picked her up from halls yesterday. He seems nice enough." She was surprised how unconvinced she sounded.

The truth was, Anne thought Josh was a drip. Tall and rangy, he was dressed in a pink Fair Trade T-shirt and baggy orange trousers that Hakim took for his PJs. Anne could just about make out fine cheekbones and a handsome face under a black bushy Peter Sutcliffe beard. He spoke with a well-to-do Scottish accent. Apparently, he'd attended Gordonstoun.

"If I were his parents, I'd ask for a refund," she'd said to Hakim in bed that night.

He glanced at her over his Vikram Seth novel. "You're sounding more like your mother every day."

"Bugger off."

He put his book down. "I don't like his choice of trousers, but Josh seems very kind and considerate. Unlike Nathan Grainger, I think he'll look out for Meg, which is exactly what she deserves."

Anne wiped a snowflake from the end of her nose. The snow was descending gently now and falling in small and finer flakes that took longer to land.

"How's Nathan doing?" she asked, feeling obliged to enquire after talking so much about Meg.

"He's not been home once all term. I guess that must mean he's having fun." Michelle looked down at her watch. "Good to see you, pet. I'd better dash, though. God knows how long it's going to take me to drive to the hospital in this weather."

The rest of the day sped by in Clay Corner. A ten-year-old burst into tears when she dropped and smashed her painted plate, and the group celebrating the fortieth birthday got very loud and squiffy after smuggling Prosecco in in their handbags. Anne had to practically push them out of the door at closing time.

It was seven by the time all the pots, mugs and vases had been varnished and put in the oven. After they'd scrubbed the tables and floors, Anne poured herself a cup of mulled wine and sat at the table by the window, cashing up. Meg joined her with a berry smoothie, and they turned up the radio to listen to the Christmas carols on Classic FM. Outside the window, snow glistened on the rooftops in the late evening sun, the sky was navy velvet and well-heeled shoppers in scarves and hats hurried along the white pavements under the Christmas lights. It was all rather enchanting.

Anne's thoughts returned to Michelle. She hadn't asked her about Billy when they'd met earlier. Eileen had told her they might be splitting up. Poor Michelle. She was totally bonkers about him. How awful if it were all to end, and in the festive season as well.

Minutes later, as if thinking about Michelle had conjured them up, Rob and Nathan walked past the window. Anne did a double take. She hadn't seen Rob since the divorce. He'd always been on the fleshy side, but he was now a mountain of a man, who took up most of the pavement. Nathan glanced casually in the window and was visibly startled to see Meg. He smiled awkwardly. Meg raised her hand and wiggled her fingers in reply.

After they'd gone, Anne eyed Meg suspiciously. "Do you ever bump into Nathan in Liverpool?"

"Funny you should say that. I had an interesting encounter with him only a couple of weeks ago."

"Go on." Trying to feign casual interest, Anne looked down and carried on bagging pound coins but she bristled. The thought of Meg within twenty yards of Nathan Grainger made her come out in hives.

Meg sipped her smoothie. "I was in the student union one night, waiting for Josh, and Nathan was at the bar. He was with the rugby crowd. They were singing songs and making an awful din. I was about to get up and leave when he came over and plonked himself next to me. He was really smashed." She rolled her eyes. "He told me I was the love of his life and that he'd been a fool to let me go."

"Really?"

"He said he'd seen me around with Josh and asked what the deal with the orange trousers was and if he'd spent time in Guantanamo Bay or something. Then Josh arrived wearing the trousers. I had to laugh."

Anne smiled nervously. "And?"

Meg shrugged. "And nothing. Nathan got up and left." She leant over the table and squeezed Anne's hand. "Don't worry, Mummy, it's over. I've moved on. "

Anne wasn't so sure. She'd noticed a dreamy look on Meg's face when she was talking about Nathan. Surely she didn't have feelings for him after the abominable way he'd treated her? Or maybe was it the nostalgia and longing everyone feels for their first love? Whatever it was, it gave Anne a prickling sensation at the back of her neck and a sense of unease.

CHAPTER 13

Eileen

Eileen watched Alex weave his way confidently up the subway steps in front of her and out onto the crowded sidewalk. Dressed in two thick jumpers under a sheepskin jacket he'd found in a thrift store, and the tan Timberland boots she'd bought him for the vicious New York winter, he strode around the Manhattan streets like he owned them. Gone was the shy slouch and lowered eyes hidden under the curtains of hair. Now, it was clipped close to his head in a buzz cut, and his expression was expectant and open. Earlier, Eileen had watched him buy their rail tickets with the ease of a local. She had wanted to laugh when he'd told the woman behind the counter to "Have a nice day". Who was this confident young man by her side? Had someone swapped him with the shy and unassuming boy that she and Sergio had waved off at Manchester airport a few months before?

Shannon had picked her up at JFK the day before and driven her through the snow-drenched suburbs to Freeport, the well-to-do Long Island suburb where she and Madison lived. As they drove through tree-lined streets, past grey and blue detached clapboard houses with multiple cars in the driveways and perfectly decorated porches full of festive wreaths and flowers, Eileen felt like she was on the set of a *Desperate Housewives Christmas Special*.

Shannon lived in a modest, less perfect-looking townhouse that backed onto the water. Her boat was docked nearby and her porch crammed with waterproof jackets, deck shoes, buoys, winch handles, and life jackets. Eileen guessed she'd chosen to live in Freeport to be close to the water. It was a lovely area, but she'd always imagined Shannon somewhere edgier, somewhere with street art on every corner, converted warehouses, and food trucks. Like Brooklyn or Harlem.

If Long Island resembled the film set of *Desperate Housewives*, then Manhattan was straight out of *Sex in the City*. Like most first-time visitors to New York, Eileen felt a sense of déjà vu as she wandered the streets. She saw scenes she'd seen countless times on TV and cinema screens. It all felt foreign but familiar at the same time. The constant beeping of car horns, the sharp accents of shouty street vendors, the queues of yellow taxis – she soaked it all up in wonder and awe. Alex laughed as, every now and again, she stopped and craned her neck to look up at the skyscrapers. He pointed out things of interest, and regularly turned to her to check she was OK, like a parent on a day trip with a giddy child. She still couldn't quite believe he was living and working here – a journey that had started back in April, on a Skype call to Shannon.

Eileen had been staring up at the slate-grey Manchester sky outside her window, while Shannon recounted how she and Madison and a couple of her friends had just come back from a boat trip to a seafood restaurant on Fire Island for her birthday. It was twenty-eight degrees and sunny, she said.

"It's far from boats and fancy restaurants you were raised," said Eileen, smiling and imagining for the umpteenth time how her life might have turned out if she'd gone to New York with Shannon when they were younger.

Their conversation gradually turned to Alex, and how he was working long day shifts in Tesco as well as doing a bar job, to save up to go travelling.

"He's considering Thailand," Eileen said.

"Why doesn't he come over to us?"

"Are you serious?"

"We'd love to have him. Madison especially. They talk all the time on social media. He could get a job in a bar or a restaurant."

"But what about papers? Isn't it impossible to get a working visa these days? I thought Trump was clamping down on that sort of thing."

"He is but there are still loads of Irish working cash-in-hand here without papers. As long as he doesn't overstay his visitor's visa, he'll be fine."

"Really?"

"Yes. U.S. Immigration are after far bigger fish than an English boy with an Irish passport. He does have one, doesn't he?"

"Of course."

"If you're worried, apply for a J1 working visa. You can only try, right?"

Alex had been ecstatic about the idea, so try they did. Within days, they'd sent off the forms then forgot all about them, not thinking for one minute they were in with a chance. In September, Alex got an email back saying he'd been successful. By mid-October he was on an American Airlines flight to JFK, having paid every penny for the trip himself. Within a week of arriving, he had a kitchen-porter job in an Italian restaurant in Freeport and he was volunteering one day a week at the hospital where Shannon worked.

Eileen and Sergio had sat back and watched him in awe. They'd marvelled at his resilience. Two years earlier, he'd been floored by PTSD, but somehow he'd managed to pull himself to his feet and change his life around.

As they exited the subway into the dazzle of Times Square, Eileen grabbed Alex and took a selfie. It was five in the morning in Manchester, but she sent it to Sergio anyway with a message.

"Alex struts around Manhattan like he's lived here all his life. Wish you were here to see him xxx"

Despite the bone-chilling cold, she was determined to see some of Manhattan on foot. After Times Square, they visited Wall Street and the Stock Exchange, then on to City Hall, followed by Broadway in a flurry of snow. As they approached the Empire

State Building, the sky suddenly darkened, giving it an eerie, otherworldly look. Tired and hungry, they stopped at a sandwich bar across the road.

Besuited office workers sat on high stools sipping coffee and eating enormous bagels, their faces buried behind copies of the *New York Times* and the *New York Post*. Eileen baulked at the prices, but Alex said one plate of chili cheese nachos between them would be plenty. He recommended the hot chocolate.

It was the first time they'd had the chance to sit down and talk properly since she'd arrived as he'd been working at the restaurant.

"Are you and Dad still fighting?" he asked, sipping from his steaming mug.

She winced and swallowed a spoonful of whipped cream. "Not so much now he's working at the deli. He seems much happier. He's not drinking or smoking as much either, as he has to get up in the mornings."

"That's good."

"He was desperate to come too, but he couldn't get the time off and we didn't have the money, what with the expense of the new house."

"I know."

"The full planning permission is through now. We should be able to start building soon."

"Cool."

"Tell me about your volunteering at the hospital. Are you enjoying it?"

He shrugged. "I guess so."

"*I guess so.*" She slapped his arm playfully. "Jesus, would you listen to the Yank. So, what exactly do you do there?"

"I turn over the patients' rooms and cubicles, sanitize the area, and change the sheets. Sometimes, I chat to the patients while they're waiting for the doctor. I help out in the emergency area as well. Lots of the patients are Hispanic and their English isn't great, so I use my Spanish to translate."

"That's fantastic." She beamed. "Dad will be so chuffed when I tell him."

A bearded twenty-something in a suit approached and asked if he could take one of the chairs from their table. Eileen caught the faint trace of an Irish accent buried under a pile of New York vowels and consonants, and she noted the expensive watch on his wrist. She wondered where he was from, what his story was, and whether he'd realised his American dream.

Alex scooped up some chili with a nacho chip. He'd been right to suggest sharing. It was an enormous portion that could have fed a family of four and two hungry dogs.

"Meg facetimed me the other night," he said.

"That's nice."

"It was. We haven't spoken for a while."

Eileen pulled a napkin from its holder. "Anne told me she has a new boyfriend. I don't think she's too impressed. Apparently he's a vegan hippie like Meg. Do you ever hear anything from Nathan?"

Alex blushed. "Meg said he's getting a bit of a name for himself at Liverpool."

"In what way?"

"Winding up the woke crowd, apparently. Posting things up on social media that have upset people."

"What type of things?"

He shrugged. "No idea. I don't follow him. Probably right-wing stuff, knowing him."

Eileen sighed. She doubted Michelle knew anything about it. Or, if she did, she wasn't saying. The poor love had enough on her plate what with Billy and his shenanigans. She wondered if she'd confronted him about the incident at the Spread Eagle yet.

In the afternoon, they made their way to Battery Park, where they picked up the ferry to the Statue of Liberty, followed by a tour of the Ellis Island Immigrant Museum. As they passed through the cavernous halls listening to their audio guides, Eileen pictured her great-aunts and uncles who had disembarked there almost a century before. She closed her eyes and imagined she was walking in their tattered boots, feeling their exhaustion and excitement after the six-day passage. How terrified they must have been as they went through medical checks, eye tests and mental examinations, worrying they might fail and be sent back. She lingered at the Kissing Point in the Great Hall, the place where successful immigrants would meet family members already settled in the US, many they'd probably never even met. They must have been so happy to see them, but also numb with heartache for those they'd left behind.

She looked around for Alex. He was standing next to a group of Italian tourists reading a plaque on one of the walls. It was clear to her that he had fallen in love with New York. Shannon had told her he was already talking about ways to extend his visa. What if he stayed forever? Eileen thought about the bittersweet feelings her own parents must have felt when she left Ireland to live in Spain and the sadness of the families of the thousands of immigrants who'd come through these halls. Whether economically or politically forced, or a choice, the act of immigration was always fraught.

She felt a pang of sadness at the thought that Alex might choose to live the rest of his life thousands of miles away from her, like a stone dropping on to her heart. She quickly banished the idea to the back of her mind. They were having the most fabulous day together, and she wasn't going to let anything spoil it.

CHAPTER 14

Michelle

The journey to work had been treacherous. When Michelle parked at the hospital, snow was still falling in hasty flurries and there were patches of black ice everywhere. She was dreading her Saturday-night shift later. Along with the usual flood of UDIs (unidentified drunken injuries), they could expect an avalanche of fractures, sprains, and broken limbs caused by the weather.

She stopped by the bereavement office to sign a couple of death certificates. As she was passing by the hospital shop, she spotted her old friend and colleague, Amir, in the queue. She hadn't seen him for ages. Seeing him standing there with his head pooled into his phone made an involuntary smile spread across her face.

He looked up, startled, as she tapped him on the shoulder.

"All right, McGreevy?" He grinned and ran his fingers through his hair. "Long time no see."

She and Amir had met in their first week as med students at Manchester University. Within days, they'd discovered they had lots in common. They were the only Mancunians on their course, they had both been brought up in working-class immigrant households, and they shared a similar dark sense of humour and a love of prog rock.

Home for Amir was a cramped terraced house in Rusholme that he shared with his Punjabi-speaking parents and five siblings. A boffin with a passion for medicine from a young age, he stood out in their student cohort like an orchid in a field of wildflowers. He politely challenged the lecturers, passed every exam with flying colours, and shone on all his placements. He'd gone on to do great things, as she always knew he would, completing a PhD in pulmonary diseases, and becoming internationally respected in his field of research.

He slipped his phone into the pocket of his scrubs and frowned. "I was just reading an email from a friend. She's a consultant in respiratory, in Beijing."

Michelle shook her head and smiled. "Forever the swot, Amir. I might have known you weren't on Facebook."

He pushed his John Lennon glasses up his nose. "Seriously, McGreevy. This sounds bad. She is doing a report about something going on in the province of Wuhan. Symptoms similar to pneumonia. Dozens of cases in a small area, with recurring hospitalisation. No aetiology."

"No aetiology?"

"Possibly linked to an animal market."

"Crikey."

"Nobody's seen anything like it."

After he'd paid for a sandwich and a KitKat, they walked along the corridor in the direction of the stroke ward.

"How's tricks with you anyway?" he asked.

"Same old. Still working in A&E. Oh, and Nathan's gone to Liverpool uni."

"No way? Where did those years go? What's he studying?"

"Have a guess."

He stared at her, wide-eyed. "Not medicine?"

She nodded.

"The lad wants his head seen to."

"Tell me about it."

They slowed down as they approached the lift.

"Sorry to hear about you and Rania, by the way," she said tentatively.

Rania had been Amir's childhood sweetheart and a student at Manchester too. They'd married in Amir's second year and now had two adult children. Michelle always thought of them as one of those solid couples you could never imagine splitting up. She had been shocked to hear Rania had left Amir for someone else.

Amir shrugged, his eyes full of hurt. "Onwards and upwards, eh?"

They stopped in front of the lift door.

"I heard you've got yourself an Irish fella," he said.

Blushing, she pressed the lift button. "I'd love to stop and chat, but I have to visit a relative on the stroke ward." As the doors opened, she stepped inside and said, "Text me and we'll go out for a drink and a catch-up, OK?"

Michelle didn't need to look at Jimmy's notes to know he was a very sick man, but she knew the nurse on duty and asked if she could have a quick look anyway. She was right, the diagnosis wasn't good. Haemorrhagic stroke, paralysis along the left side, and severe speech impairment.

He was sleeping. His bed was at the end of the packed ward, by the window. Michelle opened her card then put it next to the only other one on the bedside table, a Mass card from Jimmy's sister, Michelle's Aunt Teresa in Belfast.

Jimmy was only in his sixties, but he looked like a shrivelled man of eighty. His beard was knotted and snowy-white, his head polished, and his emaciated frame took up hardly any space in the bed. Years of loneliness and drinking had hollowed out his cheeks, jaundiced his skin, and carved out lines on every inch of his face. The nurse had told her he'd been drifting in and out of consciousness all day.

Michelle pulled up a chair and glanced around at the cards, fruit and chocolate on the other bedside tables. Jimmy had no children and hadn't had a partner in years. Rob had been right about him not getting many visitors. Apart from herself and maybe her brother Davey, she couldn't think of anyone else who would come. Even on his death bed, Jimmy was still paying the price for what he'd done when he was eighteen years old.

She moved her chair closer to the bed and put her hand on his.

He opened his glacial blue eyes. "Michelle," he whispered.

She touched his forehead. "*Shhh* ... Don't try and talk, Jimmy. I'm just going to sit here with you for a while."

As he drifted off again, Michelle was flooded with memories from her childhood.

Her dad, Paddy, had eight siblings, and Jimmy was the youngest. He left Belfast for London shortly after he'd turned eighteen. It was the mid-70's, and he worked as a joiner all over north London, frequenting the Irish pubs and clubs in Kilburn and Cricklewood. Jimmy's visits to Manchester were a highlight of her childhood. Devilishly handsome, with white-blonde, shoulder-length hair, he'd burst through the door in flamboyant shirts, bellbottom jeans and platforms, like a Bay City Roller storming the stage. He'd sit her, Davey and Tommy in a row on the floor, and read the jokes page from the *Ireland's Own* in funny voices. He was great at impressions. His Brian Clough and Harold Wilson were easily as good as Mike Yarwood's. Sometimes, he'd adopt the persona of a strict teacher called Mr Paisley, checking the pronunciation of the Belfast words he'd taught them on his last visit, words like *buck eejit* and *wee dander*. On Saturdays, he and Dad would go to watch United in the Stretford End, and on Sundays after Mass he'd take her and her brothers to Etchell's newsagent's to buy bags of Flying Saucers, Sherbet Lemons, and Curly Wurlies. The house was alive whenever he visited.

Dad was the person Jimmy called from Holloway when he was arrested for the bombing. The whole family were reeling from the shock of the news when the police broke down the front door in the middle of *Coronation Street* and took Dad away for questioning. Terrified, they all slept together that night and waited for his return. He came back at dawn with a purple bruise on the side of his face and swollen eyes. When he saw them, all curled up in the bed, he burst into tears. It was the first time Michelle had ever seen her father cry, but not the last.

A few weeks later, he sat at the kitchen table with the *Daily Mirror* spread out in front of him staring at Jimmy's picture.

"He's just a kid," he said, shaking his head, "Never in a million years did I think he'd joined the Provos. Never."

In the days that followed, the neighbours recognised Jimmy from his visits. Someone sprayed *IRA BASTARDS* across the Ford Cortina and Tommy got into a fight at school after a lad asked him if he had a collection of balaclavas or just the one. All of them felt under threat, and for some time afterwards she felt unsafe, anxious and a target. It was like they were being punished for Jimmy's crime, and it was a terrifying episode in her childhood.

Jimmy had been captured on a security video placing a bomb in a bin outside a department store in Oxford Street. Seven people had been injured in the blast. He was also charged with conspiracy to bomb a Tube station and was a suspect in the car bombings of a number of military personnel. Dad was in the public gallery in the Old Bailey when he was sentenced to thirty years. When Jimmy's mug shot was all over the *Mirror* again the next day, her mum, Kate, sat on the sofa wringing her rosary beads and saying she was ashamed to be Irish. She forbade Jimmy's name to be mentioned in the house ever again.

In the late 80's, Jimmy was transferred from Holloway to Strangeways in Manchester. Every Saturday morning, Dad would disappear out of the door with an old copy of the *Belfast Telegraph*, *Ireland's Own*, an *Irish Post,* and a box of Barry's tea in a carrier bag. Mum would throw him a dirty look. It was never mentioned where he was going, but they all knew.

When Michelle was older, her dad told her that Jimmy was full of remorse for what he'd done, and that he prayed for his victims every day. Jimmy also begged him to keep an eye on Davey and Tommy, saying, "Make sure they don't do anything hot-headed when they're young and ruin the rest of their lives like I did."

When she asked why Jimmy said to keep an eye only on the boys and not her, he smiled. "Because, like most women," he said, "you've had your head screwed on from a very young age."

In 2000, after Jimmy was released early as part of the Good Friday Agreement, he moved into a council flat in Bury. Mum relented and allowed him to visit but banned him again when he turned to drink. Jimmy was a snarly, self-pitying drunk. He could barely stand at the graveside at Dad's funeral, insisted on singing "Seán South from Garryowen", and was stopping the priest from getting on with the burial. "Seán South" was the story of a young Limerick man who'd given his life for Ireland when he was shot in an IRA ambush of a British Barracks. It was always Dad's song and he had a beautiful voice. Jimmy couldn't sing for washers. When he persisted with the singing, Davey lost it, grabbed him by the scruff of the neck, and told him he'd have to fuck off back to Bury if he carried on.

As she held Jimmy's mottled hand, Michelle thought about Seán South, a young lad dead way before his time, who'd been immortalised as a martyr in song. She then thought about Salman Abedi, who'd blown himself to bits at the Arena and she thought about Jimmy dying alone in his bed, with his two Get Well cards and no flowers or fruit. All three were young and idealistic, full of raging hormones and impassioned ideals, who'd ruined their lives at an early age. A frisson of fear ran through her as she recalled Nathan's brief brush with right-wing extremism. Thank God he'd moved on from all that.

A slither of light from the window suddenly landed on Jimmy's cheek. His wizened face reminded her of her dad's in his last days when the cancer was eating away at him. For a moment, Jimmy's skin looked diaphanous, like a veil had dropped over it. He let out a low moan. Searching for the first bars of "Seán South", Michelle quietly started to sing.

Anne

Anne was stirred from her slumber by the old-fashioned analogue ringtone of her mobile. As her brain moved from sleep to wakefulness, the sound transported her back to her childhood. An olive green boxy-shaped phone on the mahogany table in the hallway, her father in a beige cable-knit cardigan with the handset to his ear smiling down at her, and a feeling of safety and happiness. Waking fully, she squinted at the alarm clock. It was 5.20. She groaned. Not bloody Mummy again.

Since she'd gone into Swallowfields, her mother's mind had unravelled at an alarming rate but, unfortunately, she hadn't forgotten how to use a mobile phone. She rang at all hours of the day and night and rambled on about all kinds of nonsense. For a brief second, Anne considered not answering, but guilt got the better of her. She hadn't visited her in the Home in so long. The least she could do was give her five minutes of her time, even if she was half asleep.

The months before her mother had gone into the Home had been dreadful. She'd practically stopped sleeping and Hannah could hear her walking around the flat all night, clinking and clanking and playing Jim Reeves "Please Release Me" on full volume in the early hours. She went out without her keys, wandered around the neighbourhood in her dressing gown and slippers, and turned up at the primary school opposite at pick-up time, saying she'd come to collect her daughter Hannah (not, Anne noted, her *daughters* Anne and Hannah). She lost her balance a few times and fell in the street, took to slipping small bottles of gin and bags of lemons into her handbag from the small Sainsburys around the corner, and she told Hannah she'd been in the final of the Miss World Contest and kissed Eric Morley. Hannah was constantly on the blower, telling Anne she couldn't cope. What on earth did Hannah expect her to do? She lived hundreds of miles away. Besides, it was glaringly obvious that Hannah had always been their mother's favourite. She had been subsidising her and Bea and letting her live rent free in the flat for years, so she could jolly well look after her now that she wasn't well.

The final straw came when her mother left the bath running and water cascaded through the ceiling into the musician's flat below. It destroyed one of his violins, mercifully not the Stradivarius, and he was fully insured. She simply wasn't safe. It was a relief for everyone concerned when she finally went into Swallowfields. It was expensive, but it had lovely views over the Common, and there was ballroom dancing on Thursdays and afternoon tea on Fridays.

Hakim was lying on his back snoring contentedly as Anne held the phone to her ear. Her mother was regurgitating the same old nonsense she'd been coming out with for months.

"How could he do it? How could your father abandon us like that?"

Anne rolled her eyes and made sympathetic listening noises, but when her mother said the same thing for the fourth time, she lost it.

"*He didn't leave us, he was murdered, you silly old bat!*" she hissed, throwing her phone on the bed.

Hakim bolted upright up like Lazarus in the bed next to her then sighed. "Your mother again?"

"Sorry."

Falling back against the pillows, he went straight back to sleep.

Lucky bugger. She was wide awake, so she got up and showered. Today it was Carla's turn to open up Clay Corner, but Anne texted her, told her to stay in bed and said she'd go in instead. Only one more day to go until they closed for the Christmas holidays. She couldn't wait. Lazy days lying around in her PJs watching *Downtown* and *Morecombe and Wise* reruns with Meg and Hakim and devouring lots of yummy food and drink.

It was a brutal day as she set off down Brantingham Road in her vintage sheepskin coat, pink bobble hat, and boots. Steel-grey clouds congregated on the horizon and a fierce wind whipped around her feet. Such a pity the snow had gone. A white Christmas would have been divine. She started to feel bad for shouting at her mother earlier. It wasn't her fault that she had dementia, but the way she kept harping on about Daddy like that drove her bonkers.

A huge, inflatable Santa bounced around the garden of Number 33. Anne recalled the old Irish lady who used to live there. Tess, she was called. People said she was crazy. When Anne first moved into the road, she would often see her weeding or pruning and, whenever she said hello, Tess would lift her head shyly and smile. Tess had a daughter, Carmel. A neighbour recently told Anne that after Tess died, Carmel found out that her mother had been forced to give away her baby son in a Mother and Baby home in Ireland in the 1960's when she was a girl. Who wouldn't go doolally after that? Her garden used to be glorious, full of carnations, roses and cherry blossom. It was a travesty the way the people who owned the house now had gravelled over it.

The wind had calmed down by the time she crossed the junction at Chorlton Library. She made her way down Oswald Road past Priory Road Primary.

Meg had spent six months there before transferring to Broadoak. At the time, Broadoak was considered the best primary in Chorlton. Meg's sisters had gone there, but since then Chorlton had become a desirable place for families to live and the catchment area had shrunk considerably. Nathan and Alex got in because they lived nearby but Meg didn't. Distraught, Hakim harangued the local council for months until she did. The other Priory Road parents were put out when they found out. They gave her and Meg murderous looks at pick-up time and one day she overheard Lulu McFadden's mother mocking her accent and saying Meg had got the place in Broadoak because her posh mummy knew people in the right places in the council. Enraged, Anne had walked up to her, given her the middle finger, and told her to, *"Fuck right off!"*

As she was walking through the park towards Beech Road, the heavens opened. The rain was fierce and came down like thin silver pencils, creating pools and streams on the path. She sheltered under the large oak by the swings.

As she listened to the downpour battering the branches and leaves around her, she suddenly recalled something that had happened here in the park years before. Broadoak Primary had been closed for the day because of heavy snow. It was her day off work.

Meg was about eight at the time and Anne had offered to look after Alex for Eileen. She, Meg, and Alex headed off to the park.

Nathan was already there with his childminder, Cathy, and the other children she took care of. The park was full of excited kids having snowball fights and sledging. Someone had built an igloo and the kids were taking it in turns to go inside.

Anne was sitting on a bench close by, watching Alex pushing Meg on a swing, when she heard screaming. She turned to see a puny boy on all fours trying to get inside the igloo. Nathan was standing over him, holding him back by the hood of his coat, and raining punches down on his back. She leapt up and ran over, shouting at him to stop, but Nathan carried on pummelling. The boy's mother, a large woman, in a fur-trimmed parka, suddenly appeared. Yelling obscenities at the top of her voice, the woman put her arms around Nathan's waist, picked him up, and threw him to the ground like a piece of rotten fruit. She looked like she was going to thump him, but he managed to scramble to his feet and run. He sprinted the length of the park like a gazelle, slipping and sliding in the snow then running out of the gate and up Beech Road. No adult could catch him. His childminder, Cathy, found him later in Michelle's garden shed. Apparently, he had run away a number of times before and had made a den for himself there. Years later, around the time of her divorce, Michelle brought up the incident on a drunken night out with her and Eileen.

"I asked Nathan why he'd hit the boy and he replied that he'd pushed in front of him to try and get into the igloo. Then I asked him why he kept running away to the den. He told me he didn't like going to Cathy's house because there was nobody to play with except the babies. Then I asked him if he wasn't scared on his own in the shed. 'I'm not on my own,' he said. 'Daddy's home.' I told him not to be silly, that Daddy was at work. 'No, he isn't,' he insisted. 'I've seen him in the kitchen lots of times with a blonde lady dressed in black shiny stuff. She lies on the sofa and Daddy smacks her bottom.'"

She and Eileen were stunned into silence and Michelle never referred to the incident again. When Meg started seeing Nathan, Anne tried to forget about the incident because she felt indebted to Nathan for saving Meg's life at the arena. Yet the memory dogged her, like a filthy piece of dog muck on her shoe. There was always a niggling worry at the back of her mind that Nathan was very damaged and he might hurt Meg, which, in the end, turned out to be true.

The rain stopped and she dashed across the park to Clay Corner. She was surprised to see the shutters up and the light on in the back room. Carla must have missed her text. She shouted a cheery hello as she entered. Muffled voices and movement came from the back room. A few seconds later, the door opened, and Sergio emerged, buttoning up his white deli overall, his hairy chest exposed. Behind him, she glimpsed Carla zipping up her jeans.

Anne froze. She didn't immediately register what was happening. She stared at Sergio in bewilderment, as he hurried past her with his eyes to the floor.

Eileen

Emigration to America had played a significant part in Eileen's family history. Both her parents came from large families that were fractured in the wave of people who'd left County Mayo in the 1950's and 60's. More of their siblings had left for America than had stayed in Ireland. They had settled in Ohio, Florida and Colorado, but the majority had put down roots in the New York area. Since her trip to Ellis Island, Eileen had thought a lot about her parents seeing their siblings leave one by one, not knowing if or when they'd ever see them again.

She recalled the letters arriving when she was young. She would carefully peel the US stamps from the envelopes for her collection while her mother and father devoured their siblings' news. There were often photographs. Rows of cousins in St. Patrick's Day outfits parading on wide streets with hedges of shamrock pinned to their jumpers. Or Christmas pictures of them sitting around huge trees in seasonal jumpers. From the photos and the scraps of information gleaned from her parents, Eileen formed a picture of her American family. In her mind they were a wealthy and glamorous close-knit clan who got together regularly for weddings, christenings, and funerals and loved to party.

Some returned to Mayo in the summer. Giddy with excitement, she and Shannon would wait at Granny's house for their arrival. "*The Yanks have landed!*" they'd yell at the sight of the hire car pulling up on the gravel track outside. For the next fortnight, the pair of them would glue themselves to their cousins from across the pond, observing them like a rare species of animal, envying their cool sneakers and colourful backpacks, listening to endless stories of teen crushes from a magical place called High School, and letting them curl their hair into Farah Fawcett "bangs".

"One day I'm going to live in New York," Shannon announced, as they were waving them off at the end of one summer.

"What makes you think New York would have a langer like you?" Eileen retorted, hurt that Shannon hadn't included her in her plans,

Since she'd arrived in New York, Eileen had been wary about meeting her extended family. What if they were loud and bullish? What if they were over the top about their Irish heritage like Sinéad Foley?

Her fears were quickly allayed after spending time with her cousins Nora, Carol and Bernie. Interesting and sassy New York women around her age, they were extraordinarily welcoming, taking time out of their busy schedules to ferry her around Manhattan and find her cheap tickets to Broadway shows and tourist spots. They drove her upstate to the Catskills Mountains for a night to meet more cousins who ran a lively Irish motel there. On her return, Shannon hosted a party at her house, and even more relatives came. The snow falling outside, they talked and drank into the early hours, sharing family stories in front of the blazing fire to a soundtrack of the Pogues and the Dubliners. Despite an ocean and a culture that separated them, Eileen was starting to learn that they had more in common than what divided them.

Though he mainly hung out with Madison, Alex had struck up friendships with the younger members of his extended family too, in particular Patrick and Danny, bandana-wearing skateboarding twins, who welcomed him to their social circle at the local arts college where they were studying. They introduced him as their Spanish-Irish-English cousin, which he loved.

"Why did we never come and meet our family before?" he asked Eileen.

"Money," she replied, thinking with regret about the number of times Shannon had begged her to visit over the years.

It was Eileen's penultimate day in New York. She and Shannon were visiting her father's elderly sister, Maureen, who lived in Amityville, a twenty-minute drive from Freeport. A widow, Maureen lived alone in a modest, pale-blue clapboard bungalow with a maple tree at the end of the drive and an enormous American flag drooping from the dormer roof.

They parked up across the road from the house. As they hurried up the steps of the porch, Shannon pointed to the *Trump 2020 Build The Wall* sticker on the Ford truck in the drive.

"Brace yourself," she said. "I've saved the best until last."

Maureen's daughter, Barbara, answered the door. Short and heavy-set, her fleshy face had the soft fading beauty of a former prom queen. She greeted them in a Joan Rivers voice and, after they removed their coats and boots, she led them into the living room.

Maureen, eighty-six and wizened, was sitting in a leather recliner, with a tartan rug hugging her knees. Eileen kissed her rubbery cheek, then held her hand out to Maureen's son, Martin, who was sitting on the corner sofa, texting. Without looking up, he raised his palm like a traffic warden, leaving Eileen hovering awkwardly until he'd finished.

"Sorry about that. It's a work thing," he said, slipping the phone into the front pocket of his NYPD shirt. Standing, he gripped her hand and shook it firmly, saying, "Welcome to America!"

Shannon sat down at the opposite end of the sofa to Martin, and Eileen slipped into an armchair beside Maureen. Barbara asked what they would like to drink, then disappeared into the kitchen.

The room had a musty smell. Dark wood panelling covered the walls, and an enormous burnt-oak dresser stood next to the fireplace. The shelves of the dresser were busy with Christmas cards, a snow globe of an Irish cottage and a number of family photos. Pictures of JFK, the Sacred Heart, and a large photo of Teresa's late husband Tommy in his NYPD uniform adorned the walls.

Eileen had no memory of Barbara in Mayo as a child, but she had vague memories of Martin as a skinny blonde boy chasing sheep on their grandparents' farm. He was only couple of years younger than her and Shannon, but he looked much older. A wisp of a man, he had a bald polished head and a mosaic of wrinkles that spread out from his unsmiling eyes and mouth. Shannon had mentioned earlier that he'd been through an acrimonious divorce and now lived with his adult son, an opioid addict, who'd been in and out of rehab for years, which could quite well account for the wrinkles.

Barbara arrived with a tray containing bottles of Coors Light, tea, and biscuits.

"Thanks for driving all the way over to meet me," said Eileen, taking a beer. Barbara and Martin lived forty miles away on the other side of Long Island.

"No problem," replied Barbara. "We're often over this way visiting Ma."

"Not that often," sniffed Maureen.

"We do what we can." Barbara rolled her eyes and handed her mother a mug of tea.

Maureen had been the first of her father's family to leave Ireland for America sixty years before. She spoke in a heavy New York accent but every now and again, an Irish word or expression would surface and it was like hearing familiar notes in an unfamiliar song.

Eileen had read somewhere that immigrants only ever acquire the accent of the host country if they had a desire to belong. Maureen's strong New York accent seemed to be proof of this. Why wouldn't she want to belong here in New York? Hadn't America had always been good to the Irish and welcomed them with open arms? Whenever Eileen was back in Mayo, she was sometimes told her own accent had become anglicised. She baulked at the idea. She couldn't hear it herself. In all her years living in England, she wasn't sure she'd ever truly belonged.

"When were you last in Ireland, Maureen?" she asked.

"Twenty years ago." She waved a tiny hand in the air. "I'm far too old to travel now. I won't see Ireland again."

Eileen searched her face for misty eyes or traces of sentimentality but found none.

"I'm moving back," Eileen said. "We're building a house near my parents."

"You don't like England?" Maureen bit into a cookie the size of her face.

Eileen shrugged. "My husband is Spanish. It's not the same for us after Brexit."

Martin cupped his Coors bottle with both hands and leaned forward. "But you had an immigration problem. It needed to be solved, and your guy Boris Johnson solved it, right?"

Eileen laughed nervously. "Ah, Johnson wouldn't be my guy, now, Martin."

"But you have immigrants flooding in from all over Europe. Your infrastructures can't cope. Your health care system is a mess."

"At least they've got one," piped up Shannon from the corner of the room.

Martin threw her a filthy look. They'd barely spoken since they arrived. Eileen sensed the mutual dislike filling the room like a bad smell.

She gulped her beer. "The National Health Service in the UK couldn't function without foreign workers, Martin. It needs them."

Martin put his beer down and grabbed another. "But you need to control your borders just like we do. Got to build that wall."

Barbara nodded enthusiastically. "Yeah, got to build that wall!"

Eileen's mouth dropped open. She didn't know where to look.

Maureen turned to her. "Can you believe this shite?" she said quietly. "And their own mother an immigrant?"

"It's different, Ma," said Barbara sharply. "The Irish who came over here always worked. They never asked for handouts, and they didn't bring any crime with them either. The immigrants today are not the same."

Maureen sat up. "My hole, the Irish didn't bring any crime! Plenty were illegal and some were gangsters. They'd rob you as soon as look at you!" She stared into her mug. "Sure, immigrants are only people at the end of the day. Some are good, and some are bad." She looked at Martin and sniffed. "It's just the ones with black and brown faces that you and that eejit Trump don't like."

Martin frowned. "They want a free ride, that's why."

A bruising silence followed, then Barbara leant over and tapped her mother's speckled hand.

"No more politics, Ma." She looked around the room. "Anyone want another beer?"

When Eileen and Shannon left an hour or so later, the snow was falling heavily and the truck windscreens were covered with it.

"Jesus!" Eileen whispered, with a jerk of her head towards the house.

Shannon passed her an ice-scraper. "I did warn you," she muttered as they both got to work. "Martin attends all of Trump rallies here in New York, and Barbara is a big cheese in a Catholic Pro-Life organisation."

"Are you serious?"

"They both protested about same-sex marriage when the bill went through in 2011. Why do you think I haven't brought Alex to meet them?"

"God."

"Maureen's a gas, though, isn't she?"

"Oh, she's the best."

A pale-yellow moon hovered in the night sky as they hopped in the truck and set off for Freeport. Eileen couldn't wait to call Sergio and tell him about her evening. He hadn't answered the last few evenings she'd called, and she was missing him.

When they were halfway down Maureen's Street, a car honked beside them. It was Martin.

Eileen looked at Shannon, open-mouthed. "He's driving? But he's had at least five beers. And he's a cop."

Shannon shrugged. "Welcome to America."

CHAPTER 15

Michelle

Michelle sniffed and stared down into her tumbler of Negroni. "I can't believe he said those things. To think them is one thing, but to say them is another."

Eileen put an arm around her shoulder. "Tell us what happened, pet."

It was Christmas morning. The veg prepped and the turkeys left in the care of the other family members at home, Michelle, Anne and Eileen had escaped to the Horse and Jockey for a pre-dinner drink. An open fire crackled beside a huge tree, bar staff smiled in Santa hats, and Slade's "Merry Xmas Everybody" pulsed in the background.

Michelle felt anything but festive. She was still reeling after her visit to Billy, the scene playing over and over in her head like a broken film reel on a dilapidated projector. She'd hardly slept since and she'd almost burst into tears in the middle of a meeting at work just thinking about it. She'd managed to wangle both Christmas and Boxing Day off work and she fully intended to spend her time in an alcoholic stupor, which was ironic considering what she was about to tell the girls.

She twirled her drink around her glass and gulped some. "I suppose I first started to notice that things weren't quite right around the end of October. He started ignoring my texts and making excuses not to meet up. Then, he finally agreed to see me at his place the day before yesterday. When I arrived, I thought he wasn't actually going to answer the door, but then I saw movement behind the living-room curtain, so I yelled through the letterbox that I was going nowhere until he let me in. When he finally answered, I was shocked. He looked a right state. He'd lost a lot of weight, and he was barefoot, in a filthy Pogues T-shirt and jogging bottoms. His face was gaunt and jaundiced, and he couldn't look me in the eye."

A loud burst of laughter suddenly erupted from the family on the next table, momentarily interrupting Michelle's flow.

She frowned and continued. "Of course Billy had told me he was an alcoholic. I can spot an alcoholic a mile away. My Uncle Jimmy was a drunk and I've met too many to count at work." She glanced at Eileen. "I knew then that it *was* Billy that Sergio saw being taken into the police van that night outside the Spread Eagle."

She'd followed Billy into his kitchen, the smell of whisky hitting her hard. Pungent and musky, like smoky peat. When she was young, her dad took her to visit Jimmy in his dingy council flat a couple of times. The same stench permeated every room. It crawled into her pores, and she couldn't wait to leave. Billy's perfume had always been black coffee, apple-scented aftershave and his own intoxicating pheromones. He didn't wear alcohol well.

"We sat in his cesspit of a kitchen. Dirty dishes, half-opened jars and cans were strewn everywhere, and a row of empty Jack Daniel's bottles stood next to the overflowing bin." She shook her head. "I used to tease him for being so house-proud and pristine."

Eileen gave her a concerned look. "Where was Will?"

"In Galway with Bridget. Billy asked his sister over there to have them for the holidays. God knows how Will had been coping living with his dad before that. Anyway, as we sat down at the table, Billy apologised for not replying to my calls and texts and for not explaining what was going on. He pointed at the empty whisky bottles and said I didn't have to be Inspector Clouseau to work out that he'd fallen off the waggon."

"Did you tell him Sergio had seen him that night?" asked Anne.

Michelle nodded. "He said he couldn't remember a thing except waking up in the police cell the next day. He had no idea he'd gone on the rampage and tried to smash the place up."

"Gosh," said Anne. "He must have been in a very dark place to do that. Was there some kind of trigger?"

"I'm coming to that bit." Michelle reached for her glass and sipped. "Billy gave up drinking the day Julie, his ex, died. He once told me that if he ever touched a drop again, he'd never stop. At the end of October, on the third anniversary of her death, Bridget came home from Glasgow, and he and Bridget and Will had a nice day together. After the kids were in bed, he got out some old photo albums. He said he'd never looked at them since Julie died. As he flicked through the memories of their life together, he said it struck him for the first time that he was never going to see her again. Apparently, he'd never fully accepted it before."

"Really?" Eileen pulled a sceptical face.

"I get that," said Anne. "People grieve differently and at their own pace."

Michelle sighed. "To numb the pain, he went out and bought a bottle of Jack Daniel's and a bottle of cheap red, then drank the lot. After that, he went on a three-day bender and ended up at the Spread Eagle.

"Golly," said Anne. "Three days."

"He said he'd buried the pain of Julie's death before that by throwing himself into things, going full pelt, keeping busy with work and the kids, and other distractions." Michelle swallowed. "I took that to mean me."

"Ah now," said Eileen, "I'm sure he didn't mean that."

"Didn't he? Anyway, then he started rambling on about himself in that annoying self-pitying way drinkers do. He said he wasn't the man I thought he was, that he was an alcoholic who'd barely been holding it together since his wife died, that he was a useless father and a pathetic loser. Not once did he mention me or our relationship. The more he talked, the more I realised how little I'd meant to him. He, on the other hand, had been the centre of my world. It was like he'd been leading a double life when we were together – his real, deeply troubled one, and the one he'd lived with me where he pretended everything was OK. I finally plucked up the courage to ask him what part I'd played in all of this." Her voice cracked. "I still can't believe what he said."

Eileen put a hand on hers. "Go on."

"He said I reminded him of Julie the moment he saw me on the dating app: the hair, the face, the build. He said I even had the same accent and feisty spirit."

"The rotter," said Anne.

Eileen's jaw dropped. "He did not say that."

"He did. I was gobsmacked. I asked him if I was some kind of replacement for his dead wife, and if he was fucking her whenever we had sex. He didn't answer and he didn't look at me. Then I asked if he'd felt anything for me at all." She wiped her eyes. "He said he respected and admired me a lot. Especially for the way I dealt with Nathan and my dedication to my job." She shook her head. "Respect and admiration. That's what he felt for me all the time we were together. Well, I loved the bones of him. More than I've ever loved anyone."

She lifted her glass high in the air and threw her head back. "Merry fucking Xmas and a Happy New Year!" she said. "Good riddance, 2019! Here's hoping 2020 is a better one."

PART FIVE

CHAPTER 16

Three months later

March, 2020

Michelle

"Middle of March?" The cab driver gestured into the empty street. "More like Christmas Day. It's as dead as a doornail out there."

"It's mad, isn't it?" Michelle sat back in her seat.

"I'm hoping it'll all be over by the end of the month. I've got a holiday booked in Tenerife."

"I wouldn't count on it." She recalled telling her team that all leave was suspended for three months. They'd all looked at her like she was the Wicked Witch of the West.

The driver glanced at her in his rear-view mirror. "What do you do then? Do you work at the courts?"

"No. I was there for an inquest. I'm an A&E doctor at the Infirmary."

He let out a low whistle. "Respect. I wouldn't have your job for all the money in the world right now."

"Cheers." Michelle smiled and leant her head against the windowpane. She'd found a puncture in her front tyre that morning, so she'd got a cab to and from the courts. No way was she risking a bus or a tram. She'd sat in the back away from the driver's seat and opened the window too. She sighed. What was the point? Tomorrow, she'd be back at work, inches from coughing and spluttering mouths, her only protection a flimsy paper mask, or a visor made by school kids in an art class.

They passed through Oxford Road. The university area was one of the busiest parts of the city. Normally the streets would be crammed with cars and buses, the pavements bustling with young people heading into fast-food joints and lectures. Now it was a ghost town. Most of the students had gone home, and instead of posters advertising gigs and protests, the windows in the cafés and bars were filled with *Temporarily Closed* and *Stay Safe* signs. The silence was unreal, broken only by the sound of a passing car or the wail of an ambulance heading for the nearby Infirmary. The streets in the university area in Liverpool had a similar vibe when she'd picked Nathan up the day before.

He had a face like thunder, and he'd barely said a word as they piled all his stuff into the car. They'd been driving for about five minutes when he started kicking the footwell.

"*Fuck it*," he growled. "I don't want to come back home."

"I know. It's hard for you kids," she replied.

"It's all probably one big conspiracy to take away our freedom anyway."

Waiting until it was safe, Michelle pulled over and turned off the ignition. "Looks like someone's been talking to their dad," she said.

He stared sullenly at the rain-spattered windscreen and said nothing.

She took a couple of deep breaths. "Nathan, if you genuinely believe Covid 19 is some kind of Bill Gates plot created by the globalist elite to suppress the masses, then you'd better give up studying medicine right now."

He chewed the side of his cheek.

She continued, "I mean it. This is a global pandemic and it's as real as it gets. You might want to listen to me on this one and not your dad."

He sighed theatrically. "Of course I believe it's real."

"Glad to hear it."

"I'm just pissed off at having my life interrupted before it's even begun."

He shook his head slowly. "I cannot believe the Blossoms gig got cancelled. I was so looking forward to it."

The cab slowed to a halt at Asda in Hulme. Cars were snaking around the block to get into the packed car park. She'd read in the

Manchester Evening News that they'd put security guards on the aisle where the toilet rolls were kept after customers had fought to get at them. On the pavement outside the cab window, a blue plastic glove fluttered in the breeze. They littered the streets these days, like diseased birds fallen from the sky. Funny how the general public could get hold of items of PPE so easily when the hospital couldn't. The nurses on her ward were making aprons out of bin bags and the surgical mask she'd been given was useless because it was made for a male jaw.

They passed a primary school in Whalley Range at pick-up time. Michelle shuddered at the sight of a young girl running up to her elderly grandparents and hugging them. SAGE, the Scientific Advisory Group for Emergencies, had told Boris Johnson weeks ago that closing schools could cut transmission by fifty percent, yet he'd done nothing. He was far too busy shaking hands with Covid patients on hospital wards to take any notice.

Michelle had become obsessed with the stats, waking at all hours, reaching for her phone and checking the daily toll of cases, deaths, ages of patients, and location. The first death in the region had been recorded at North Manchester General a few days before. A man in his 60's, with underlying health conditions, had contracted the virus in Italy. She devoured every podcast and *Lancet* article that Amir, her old friend and colleague, sent to her. She remembered the day she bumped into him when she was visiting her Uncle Jimmy at the hospital. He'd been reading about the early reports coming from Wuhan then. Trust Amir to be on to it before anyone else. Jimmy had died a couple of days later. It was a godsend really. At least he wouldn't be lying on a ward caught up in all of this.

That morning, she'd seen a report on Sky News from a hospital in Bergamo, in Northern Italy. The intensive care wards were at breaking point. She'd watched with her heart in her mouth, as staff heaved dying patients over on their stomachs to take pressure off their lungs, doctors and nurses slumped on floors after twelve-hour shifts, and coffins lined a makeshift mortuary in an adjacent building.

Afterwards there was an interview with an Italian neurosurgeon who'd been transferred to work on a Covid ward. The woman had been desperate to get her message across. "Don't think that it's happening here, and it can't happen anywhere else," she'd said in faltering English. "*Do something. Act now.*"

And what was happening here? Boris et al were dithering and procrastinating about herd immunity. She and every medical professional she knew were raging. The refusal to lock down would cost thousands of lives.

Anne had recently sent her a video of Italians singing on their balconies weeks into their lockdown. Banners surrounded them saying *Tutto Andra Bene* – everything will be fine. She thought about the glorious weekend she and Billy had spent in Verona the previous September, when everything *had* been fine. She still thought about him most days. Analysing their relationship, she'd come to the painful conclusion that Billy, like Rob, had been unfaithful. The fact that Billy's other woman was his late wife didn't make the betrayal hurt any less. At the end of the day,

Michelle hadn't been enough for either of them. That was it. She was done with men for the foreseeable.

As the cab pulled up outside her house in the empty street, her thoughts drifted back to work. Every morning, as she parked in the hospital car park before her shift, she felt like she was standing on a beach waiting for the first wave of a tsunami to hit. It was going to be tough, that much she knew, and she was bracing herself for the weeks and months ahead. The hardest part was having to face it alone.

Anne

The Meadows was absolutely heaving. Three weeks into lockdown, the entire population of Chorlton seemed to be taking their government-sanctioned exercise on the paths and fields. It was a tepid day, more like summer than late April and the sun warmed the nape of her neck. People were trying to keep to the two-metre rule on the crowded paths, skirting around each other, like they were doing some sort of old-fashioned dance routine they hadn't quite got the hang of. It was hilarious. Joggers were yelled at for running too fast, and cyclists given the evil eye, their sweaty airborne particles viewed as potential lethal bullets. Anne shook her head. The world had gone stark raving bonkers.

After she'd been walking for about ten minutes, she spotted Eileen strolling on the path ahead of her under a line of willow trees with her pooch, Rory. She looked gorgeous in a short floaty red dress and sturdy walking boots that accentuated her long legs.

Anne felt uneasy. She'd seen Eileen twice since she'd caught Sergio and Carla in flagrante that morning at Clay Corner. It was irrational, but both times she couldn't shake off her discomfort and guilt, like *she* was the one who'd done something wrong, not Sergio.

Eileen waved enthusiastically and headed in her direction. Rory made a beeline for her too. More of a small horse than a dog, he had a habit of jumping up at every moving object. She closed her eyes, crossed her arms tightly against her chest, and braced herself for the assault.

He jumped on her. Eileen dragged him off and apologised. Anne hated dogs.

"How's Michelle?" she asked, as Eileen was putting the beast on its lead.

"Still exhausted. She can't seem to shake off the cough."

"Shouldn't she be over it by now?"

Eileen shrugged. "I don't know what's going on there. Nathan's had it too with barely any symptoms. I've been dropping off shopping at the house. I go round the back and sit outside on the patio, and she stays behind the French windows. She opens them just enough for us to hear each other and we have a chat. Why don't you go round?"

Anne's eyes widened. "*Err* ... because it's illegal?"

"Sure, you'll be fine. Her isolation period has ended. She'd love to see you."

"Let me look in my diary and see what I've got on." Anne pretended to look at her phone. "Oh, what a surprise. I seem to be free. I might just do that later."

They turned onto a less crowded path, walking together but apart, Eileen keeping the horse on its lead.

Anne was surprised to hear that Eileen and Michelle were bending the rules and meeting up, especially as Michelle was a doctor. In every other way, they were both very strict about lockdown dictates. Anne had a friend who was wiping down her shopping before she brought it into the house. Now, that was a step too far in her book.

They walked on. The woods were blooming. Fields of bluebells appeared around every corner, cowslip and primrose were making an appearance, and she could smell wild garlic.

She fanned her face with her hand. "How's Alex doing?"

"He's grand. Everyone in the house in Freeport had the virus a few weeks ago, but they're all fine. All the staff are going off sick at the hospital where he's been volunteering, and he's been offered a job as a porter. Shannon managed to pull some strings with HR and his visa has been extended."

"That's fantastic." Anne forced a smile. "You must be so proud of him."

Eileen pulled Rory away from yet another dog whose bottom he'd taken a fancy to. "We are, but I do worry. The hospitals over there are rammed with Covid patients. He's so young. It's a lot to be taking on at his age, especially after what he went through at the time of the bombing."

"Alex is made of strong stuff. He'll be fine, darling. At least he's out there doing his bit. Lockdown is the worst thing that could have happened to Meg. She'd finally found her feet at uni and was thriving but now her anxiety is back big-time. For anxiety-sufferers like her the pandemic confirms their belief that the world is a dangerous place."

"Sorry to hear that. Poor Meg."

Anne kicked at a stone on the path in front of her. "Nobody is thinking about mental health when they're shutting the country down, especially young people's mental health. The disruption to their education and damage to their social well-being will take its toll big-time."

"But what's the alternative?"

"Sweden isn't locking down, and their death rates aren't any worse than ours. They're advising people to work from home and only putting restrictions on the vulnerable. They are being sensible. None of this blanket 'everyone has to stay at home' bullshit."

Eileen went quiet, as most people did whenever she questioned the lockdown. Anne sighed. Surely she couldn't be the only one who thought it was a load of old codswallop?

She decided to change the subject. "So, what's the news with the house in Ireland?"

"Don't ask." Eileen looked glum. She stopped by a tree to let Rory sniff it. "Everything's on hold. Lockdown is stricter over there than it is here."

"Is that even possible?" Anne shook her head. "It's all so shit, isn't it? So very *very* shit." She looked down and patted her stomach. "And we're all getting fat. I've put on five pounds. Hakim cooks yummy food every night, because there's nothing else to look forward to."

"Sergio's been kept on at Ludo, thank Christ. I'd feckin' hate it if he was at home under my feet all day."

At the mention of Sergio, Anne looked away and quickened her pace.

She'd fired Carla the day after she'd found them together at Clay Corner. Not a word was mentioned about the incident. Carla simply burst into tears, collected her things, and hurried out of the door. Anne had been loath to do it. Carla had been the best employee she'd ever had. She would be irreplaceable. But Eileen was her dear friend. How could she work alongside Carla every day, knowing she was having sex with Sergio?

He had never once approached Anne to talk about the incident. What on earth was he thinking? Was he burying his head in the sand and waiting for her to tell Eileen? Or was he confident she wouldn't? She contemplated talking to Michelle about it but telling Michelle and not Eileen felt like a betrayal. Hakim said to stay silent because it was probably a one-off, and who was she to break up a marriage? Anne suspected otherwise. Carla had been volunteering to do the early shifts for some time. Anne had an inkling there'd been many more mornings of passion by the heat of that clay oven.

After much soul-searching, Anne had decided not to tell. Keeping it from Eileen felt like a betrayal, but she knew how much she loved Sergio. They were building a new life together in Ireland and it would destroy Eileen to find out.

In late February, she'd received an email from Carla saying she'd moved back to Barcelona and wanted information about her tax status. It looked like the affair, or fling, was over and Anne immediately felt exonerated from having to tell Eileen anything.

As she and Eileen parted, she watched her walk down the sunlit path. Perhaps her decision not to tell her had been a cowardly one and she'd taken the easy route. Nevertheless, she'd made it now and was sticking by it.

After leaving the Meadows, Anne texted Michelle asking if she could come round. She immediately received an emphatic "**Yes, please**", so she headed to the shops on Beech Road to buy a little gift to cheer her up.

Socially distanced queues had formed outside the Co-op, Ludo deli, and Etchell's newsagent's, the only shops open apart from the chemist's.

Before joining the queue, Anne peeped in the window of Ludo. When she couldn't see Sergio behind the counter, she took a place. As she waited, she stared at Clay Corner amongst the row of other shuttered shops. Business had never been better these last few months, but now she wondered if the place had any future at all.

Who on earth would want to rush out and make vases and paint plates when lockdown was over? At least she'd been furloughed, though, which was something.

The large lady in front of her was wearing blue plastic gloves and a paper mask. She kept looking around, making sure everyone was keeping to the two-metre rule, like a Rottweiler marking its territory. Apart from a young Chinese couple in Morrisons, it was the first time Anne had seen anyone wearing a mask. It was pure scaremongering. There was simply no need for it.

Armed with a bottle of Bordeaux, four Danish pastries, and the feeling she was doing something improper, she headed to Michelle's house in Chorltonville. The windows of the lovely houses were plastered with drawings of rainbows and unicorns and messages thanking the NHS. Her friendship with Michelle had been pretty challenging these past few years, but every Thursday evening at clap-and-bang-your-pots time in the street, Michelle was always the person at the forefront of her mind.

When Anne arrived, she checked nobody was looking, then slipped furtively through the side gate. As she walked across the patio, she could hear coughing from behind the French windows. She had googled the Covid cough lots of times. Michelle was the first person she knew who had contracted the virus and she had to admit that hearing that dry barking sound for real was pretty damn scary. She knocked on the window, called Michelle's name, then dragged a rattan chair from the garden table. She picked up a copy of yesterday's *Guardian* that was lying there. The front page advertised an interesting-looking article about DIY haircuts.

Positioning the chair two metres from the window, she put the Ludo bag by the window, then sat down and waited.

The garden was a riot of colour. Daffodils and hydrangea lined the flower beds, along with mounds of purple crocus, hedges were perfectly trimmed, and the lawn was luscious and fresh smelling. Anne listened for the birdsong that everyone was going bonkers about. No longer drowned out by the noise of the city or made hoarse by the dirty air, the dawn chorus could apparently be heard all day, every day. Well, bugger the birdsong. She missed the sounds of the city: the rush of traffic, beeping horns, police helicopters, and drunks swearing in the street. She longed to get back to normal.

Michelle appeared inside in a blue towelling dressing gown, a pair of enormous yellow slippers in the shape of ducks and her frizz of hair standing up on her head, like she'd just been plugged in. She opened the blinds and slowly slid the door open an inch or so. Normally rosy and rotund, she looked haggard and pale. What struck Anne the most, though, was the expression on her face. She couldn't remember Michelle ever looking so down.

"You and Eileen will get me struck off with your visits," she said with a weak smile.

Anne gestured at the Ludo bag. "A little something for you."

"Thanks, pet." She sat down on an orange retro chair.

"I've just stolen your copy of yesterday's *Guardian* from the table if that's OK."

"No problem."

"How are you feeling?"

Michelle tightened her dressing gown. "I've been better."

"And Nathan?"

"Slight temperature for a day, and that was it."

"Oh, to be young!"

"Indeed."

"When are you back at work?"

"The weekend."

"You're kidding."

Michelle shrugged. "No staff. Everybody's off with the virus."

She suddenly erupted into a fit of coughing and disappeared inside.

When she returned with a glass of water, Anne could see she was struggling to keep alert, so she tried to keep the conversation as light as possible, telling her about the two shoppers in full boiler suits and gasmasks Hakim had seen in Stretford Shopping Mall.

Michelle laughed.

"It's all a bit hysterical, isn't it?" said Anne.

Michelle coughed again with her hand over her mouth and raised her eyebrows. "Hysterical?" she said.

"All of it. The lockdown, the dramatic way people are behaving. It's all a bit over the top if you ask me."

Michelle sighed. "Eileen did mention that you were sceptical." She looked past her into the garden. "My colleague Amir was brought onto the Covid ward last night. He's in a bad way and may have to go on a ventilator."

"Really?" Anne curled a lock of her hair nervously behind her ear. "How old?"

"Forty-seven and as fit as a fiddle. A marathon runner. I've known him since my uni days. Two of our nurses were admitted weeks ago as well. They came into contact with infected patients when we had no PPE. Back then Public Health England were telling us not to test the patients unless they had a travel history." She looked at Anne directly. "How's your mum? Has the care home she's in been affected?"

"A couple of cases." Anne avoided her gaze and bit her lower lip. "No deaths, though."

"You're very lucky. Infected Care Home residents have been discharged from hospitals all around the country and sent back to their Homes because the beds were needed for Covid patients. Testing them before they left took too long. I discharged one patient back to a Care Home in Didsbury myself, not knowing she was infected. Within weeks three people from that same Care Home were admitted with the virus." She swallowed. "So, in answer to your question about whether I think lockdown is hysterical, I'd say no." She got to her feet. "I'm sorry, Anne, I really don't feel well. I'm going to have to go back to bed."

Anne jumped up from her seat, her face burning. "No worries, hon. I can come back another time."

Raising her hand in a weak wave, Michelle disappeared back into the house. Anne put the chair back in its place, walked across the patio then out of the side gate, feeling like she'd just had a dressing-down from her favourite teacher.

That evening, after watching the Health Secretary and bore of the year Matt Hancock on the daily TV Covid update, Anne sat back on the sofa and reached for the newspaper she'd taken from Michelle's table. As she did so, another newspaper slipped out, its pages scattering across the sofa. It had a Gaelic-looking name. *An Phoblacht*. Michelle must have forgotten it was there. Anne gathered up the papers, drawn to a photograph on a front page. It was an old picture, probably taken in the 60's or 70's, a headshot of a young man in a wide collared floral shirt. She was taken aback. The resemblance to Nathan was uncanny. The same cheekbones, icy blue eyes, and devilish grin.

She quickly scanned the accompanying article.

REMEMBERING JIMMY McGREEVY

A memorial service was held on 9th February in St. Agnes Church in Anderstown to honour veteran Belfast republican Jimmy McGreevy, who passed away peacefully in Manchester, UK, in December at the age of sixty-six.

As a young man, McGreevy stood up against the injustices he witnessed on the streets of Belfast and throughout the North. At seventeen he moved to London where he completed active service. In 1976, he was imprisoned in various English jails for his part in a number of London bombings, including acts targeting British military personnel, as part of the struggle. Following his release as part of the Good Friday agreement, he lived a quiet life in Manchester. McGreevy's final wish was for his ashes to rest with his mother Irene and father Frank in Anderstown Cemetery. Wreaths were laid on behalf of the Republican Movement.

Seán Reilly, a former friend and comrade, had these words to say: "Jimmy McGreevy was a brave soldier who sacrificed years of his life for the cause of Irish freedom. He came from a solid Irish family tradition and will never be forgotten. I would like to take this opportunity to pass on my condolences to his siblings, nephews and nieces and remaining family in Manchester."

Anne read the article again, pausing at the sentence **"Imprisoned in various English jails for his part in a number of London bombings, including those targeting military personnel."**

When she'd bumped into Michelle on Beech Road at Christmas, Anne remembered her saying that she was going to see a sick uncle in hospital. She told her he'd died shortly afterwards. A cold shiver ran through her, making her tremble and she let the paper fall. Picking up her phone from the coffee table, she googled the name Jimmy McGreevy.

CHAPTER 17

Eileen

Eileen closed the lid of her laptop. She was exhausted after six consecutive hours on Teams. Five weeks into lockdown, she was finding online teaching pure hell. At least ten minutes of every lesson was wasted helping older students who couldn't manage the tech. Another might press the wrong button halfway through and disappear from the screen, and sometimes a pet or child or a half-dressed housemate would appear, causing mayhem for everyone. Some refused to put their cameras on at all. Teaching a black square was just fecking bizarre.

Many of her younger students had been working in the hospitality sectors to fund their courses, so as soon as the bars and restaurants had closed, they'd got on a plane and gone home. Eileen had become attached to them, and it was heart-breaking to see them go. Those who stayed were cooped up in rooms in empty student halls of residence, worrying about their families, thousands of miles away. Some were as young as seventeen, and mentally fragile. Eileen found herself increasingly taking on the role of substitute parent and counsellor in the lessons. Grammar and writing skills went out the window, as her students offloaded their fears and anxieties. Only a few days before, she'd had to contact the emergency services about Jia, a smart Taiwanese student, who said she'd been hearing voices. She was beginning to think Anne was right when she'd said in the Meadows that lockdown would have a disastrous effect on young people's mental health. Shutting them inside at such a crucial stage in their development was contrary to human nature. Yet the old and the vulnerable couldn't be left to die. What else could anyone do until there was a vaccine?

She stared out at the estate from the window of her box-room turned classroom. After a fortnight of sunshine, the weather had turned. Today was a soft April day. Drizzle dropped over the rows of identical slate rooves, and silver puddles shone in the streets, like large mirrors. She liked lockdown. She revelled in the quiet of it, not realising how accustomed she'd become to the twenty-four-seven noise on the estate until now: the thud of music from car stereos, burglar alarms, roaming kids shouting and roaring, and arguments through open windows.

A month in, people were getting restless. From her watchtower, she'd spied small gatherings on street corners, and friends and family going in and out of each other's houses again. Yesterday, she spotted her next-door neighbour Mary Porter's teenage granddaughters sneaking in her back gate. Mary was a fearless Glaswegian, who smoked twenty Silk Cut a day and had chronic lung disease. Eileen had to restrain herself from opening the window and yelling, *"Don't kill your granny!"* It wouldn't have made a blind bit of difference. Mary had told Eileen no-one was stopping her seeing her family, least of all that fat fuck Boris

Johnson. She didn't give a toss if he was in intensive care, either, she said. He could die for all she cared. He was a Tory twat, who only looked after his own.

Eileen went downstairs to make dinner. Her wartime supply of pasta was running out. She needed to go to Aldi. The thought of a trip to the supermarket made her giddy. She might be a real devil and ask Michelle or Anne if they fancied meeting in the socially distanced queue for a chat. Never had the big shop been fraught with so much excitement. She glanced at the wall clock. Sergio would be back from the deli soon. He finished early today so he'd be in time for Alex's Zoom call.

She and Sergio were probably one of the few couples who saw less of each other in lockdown than normal times. She taught online all day, he left for work about midday and worked until late, so they only had an hour or so with each other when he got in. She didn't mind. His mood had improved dramatically now he was working, and he was happy when they'd asked him to stay on. It had been good for their relationship too. He was so sweet and attentive these days, showering her with compliments and telling her how much he loved her. She felt lucky. So many of her friends whinged about their sexless, stale marriages, and how they hated being with their partners twenty-four-seven in lockdown. Yes, she and Sergio had their ups and downs, but after twenty-five years together, they were still rock solid.

She chopped an onion, wiped her eyes, and stared out at the rain firing down on the bins in the back yard. If it wasn't for Covid, she'd be looking out of the window of her new kitchen in Mayo by now. It would probably be lashing down, but at least she'd be looking out at lush green fields and the lake. She pictured the half-built house up there on the hill, exposed to the elements, cement mixers and machinery abandoned close by, along with her hopes and dreams.

The building work had stopped as soon as the Irish lockdown was announced in early March. Construction was still permitted, but the plumbers and electricians had pulled out, making all kinds of excuses. Her father couldn't find anyone else to take over. She suspected the money-grabbing feckers had got more lucrative offers elsewhere. She was angry and frustrated, but there wasn't a thing she could do about it. Then the buyers of the Chorlton house had pulled out a week away from exchanging. Sally, the agent at Sherlock Homes, had called her with the news, citing the uncertainty surrounding Covid.

"We'll try to get more viewings, but it won't be easy," she'd said. "People are scared of committing to anything."

Eileen had been gutted. Christ knows when or if they'd sell now. Sergio, on the other hand, seemed to be taking it all on the chin.

"Give over with the long face," he'd said to her that evening after she'd burst into tears.

She'd smiled through her tears. The way he imitated her Irish colloquialisms in his Spanish accent never failed to amuse her.

"People are dying all over the world," he'd said, "but the house will still be built when this is all over."

He was right, of course. She was being a brat. Yet his lack of distress was worrying. Was he losing interest in the move?

He was always lukewarm whenever she presented him with any house-design plans or potential job opportunities. The thought that he might not want to go niggled at the back of her mind, like an itch she couldn't scratch.

She switched on the radio for the six o'clock news. Captain Tom had raised over thirty-one million for the NHS and was celebrating his hundredth birthday. How could she whinge with people like Captain Tom in the world? Trump was accusing China of manufacturing the virus, and Boris declared that the UK was past its peak. With thirty thousand dead and counting, she hoped so. Over seventy thousand dead in the US. She sliced open a box of passata and shook her head. Who could have predicted that the UK and the US would have such high death rates in a global pandemic? Proportionately, Ireland had one of the lowest. She was proud of the way her little country was conducting itself. But then it was led by a former GP, who followed the science, not a bumbling eejit or a tangerine sociopath. She mixed the sauce and pasta, added mozzarella, and put it in the oven. It was almost six-thirty – one-thirty Stateside. Alex was calling on his lunchbreak at the hospital. She made a coffee, took it up to the box-room, switched on her laptop, and waited.

She and Sergio had asked Alex to get a flight home from New York before the restrictions on international travel took effect. He'd refused as they knew he would. Despite the pandemic, he was desperate to stay. He told her recently that he'd met someone. A Dub, no less. Ross Kelly was from Howth, twenty-one, and a nurse at the hospital. Shannon described him as gentle, self-contained, and good craic and said she highly approved. Alex had sent her a photo of him with Ross at the John Lennon memorial in Central Park. They made a cute couple. Ross was a looker, with deep-set eyes, a fine head of sandy-coloured curls, and a nose-ring. Alex had so much going for him in New York: a job, a relationship, and a lockdown that wasn't nearly as strict as it was here. She accepted that he wasn't coming home any time soon.

The sight of Alex's lovely face filling her laptop screen made her grin from ear to ear. Cloudless blue skies filled the space behind his head, and a vivid red stripe was slashed across his nose where his mask had been.

"Sorry I'm late," he said.

"Where are you?"

"On the grass area at the back of the hospital. It's a beautiful day. Check out the madhouse." He positioned his phone so that she had a panoramic view of the long redbrick building behind him.

Staff in green scrubs sprawled on the grass, drinking from coffee cups and staring at phones. Others were smoking by a row of large industrial grey bins and hurrying in and out of a set of double doors. A huge white trailer was stationed along one wall. When Alex started to move the phone away, she asked him to focus it back again. Three people in hazmat suits were coming out of the double doors, wheeling a gurney carrying a red plastic bundle. A forklift operator suddenly moved into view.

Alex turned his head, moving the phone back to his face, and she couldn't see any more.

Neither of them spoke for a few seconds.

"Is that what I think it is?" she asked.

"The guys putting the body into the trailer?"

"Yes."

He nodded. "The undertakers are inundated. We have to keep the dead refrigerated in the trailers until they can take them."

"Do you have to help with any of that?"

He nodded. "Sometimes."

"Jesus."

"At least our trailer is out the back, Mum. In the city hospitals, they are on the sidewalks. People driving or walking past can see the bodies being loaded in."

"Are you serious?"

"It's tough."

"Their poor families."

Alex sipped from a can of Coke. "Most of the seriously ill in this hospital are African American or Hispanic. Some of the Hispanics have no English at all. I help facetime their families, using my Spanish."

"Oh Alex."

"It's so sad, Mum. They're dying and they're totally alone."

"It's a lot for you to take on."

She searched his face. She thought back to what he'd been through at the Arena, and the PTSD afterwards. Now he was surrounded by death on a daily basis. She didn't like it. He was far too young for all this.

"Are you getting enough sleep?" she asked.

He smiled. "The bar-hopping and clubbing in Manhattan keep me up most nights."

"Seriously, Alex. Don't take on too much. Look after your mental health."

"Stop flapping. I'm fine."

"How's Ross?"

His face brightened. "Good, thanks."

"I don't suppose you get to see much of him."

"At the hospital, if we're on the same shift. Or at weekends."

"What do you do?"

"Walk around the empty streets of Manhattan or go for a drive to Jones beach. We figured it's OK as we've both had the virus."

"Be careful you don't get arrested and deported."

He smiled. "No chance. I'm a model citizen." He threw his head back and drank more Coke. "Any news?"

"Michelle still hasn't fully recovered from the virus, but she's back at work. And Boris Johnson didn't die. Not much else to report since we last spoke."

"I heard from Meg that Nathan is in trouble at Liverpool."

"Really?"

"Something to do with exams. I don't know the details."

Eileen frowned. "Michelle never said."

"He's hardly going to tell her, is he?"

"I suppose not."

"And neither should you. Keep mum, Mum." He smiled at his own joke.

"I promise I won't say a word. Do you speak to Meg a lot, then?"

"Every week or so."

"It's nice you're pals again." Eileen tilted her head at the sound of the key in the front door. "Your dad's back. I'll put him on."

At the sound of Alex's voice, Sergio hurried upstairs. Blowing kisses at the screen, Eileen said goodbye and left the room as he came in.

She went downstairs and checked on the pasta in the oven. As she was laying the table, her phone rang on the worktop. Seeing Michelle's name on the screen, she picked it up and took it into the living room.

"Hello, you," she said, flopping on to the sofa. "How's it going?"

"I've been better," she replied, as a sudden gust of rain rattled against the windowpane. "Rob died this morning."

Michelle

Michelle had just got back after her shift when Jane called with the news. She was exhausted. Groggy and half asleep, she listened to her rambling on with the familiarity and ease of an old friend, instead of the woman who'd stolen her husband.

"I tried to warn him, Michelle," she wailed. "I said you've got your diabetes, you can't go getting this virus, you need to stay in. But would he listen? Would he hell! Lockdown was a load of bollocks, he said. He carried on going to bars and restaurants, right up until they closed, then he'd sneak off to parties."

"Parties?"

"In the villas in the hills. He probably caught it at our friend Colin's sixtieth in Benahavis. Two other people there tested positive. It all happened so quickly. He was only admitted on Monday."

"You mean he was in hospital for three days, and you never told us?"

A silence followed. "He told me not to. Said he was getting better. His oxygen levels had improved, and the last time we spoke he said he'd be out the next day. Oh, the thought of him all alone in there, with everyone gabbling on in Spanish and him not understanding a word. That's no way to go, is it?"

"Nathan could have spoken to him if you'd let us know."

"What?" Another silence, then another wail. "Oh, I don't need a guilt trip from you, Michelle! I really don't! I've just lost the love of my life, and now I'm stuck over here all on my own in this blasted lockdown. I don't even know what the rules are about funerals and burials. He said he wanted his ashes scattered in the sea in front of Healey Mac's Irish Bar. He loved it there."

Michelle had a sudden urge to laugh, and she had to put her hand over her mouth to stop herself. The thought of Rob, fanatical Brexiteer, having his ashes scattered on a Spanish beach in front of an Irish pub, was bizarre. She was appalled at her reaction, but she put it down to the shock.

Only when she came off the phone did she register the enormity of what Jane had just told her. Rob had gone and Nathan probably wouldn't be able to attend his funeral and say goodbye. There was nothing funny about that at all. Bracing herself, she headed straight up to Nathan's attic room to tell him.

She was panting when she reached the top of the stairs. She couldn't walk for any length of time now without wheezing. She was convinced the virus had damaged her lungs. She opened the door and entered.

Nathan sitting at his desk on his laptop. He turned sharply. "Ever thought of knocking?" he said, glaring at her and shutting the lid.

Fighting back tears, she gestured at him to sit down on the bed beside her.

"It's Dad," she said. "He's gone ... I mean he's passed ... it was Covid."

He stared back at her in bewilderment. "You're lying."

She closed her eyes. "I'm so sorry, Nathan."

"*You're fucking lying!*"

She reached out to touch him, but he pushed her back on to the bed then bolted downstairs and out of the front door. From the window she watched him run down the street. She felt every bit of his pain, but she was used to him taking flight when bad stuff happened. That was his way.

When he'd gone from her sight she slumped down on his bed, the joint weight of shock and grief crushing her.

Shortly afterwards she rang Eileen who said, "Stuff Covid, I'm coming over."

"I'd love that more than anything, pet," she replied. "But Nathan did a runner when I told him. He's not taken his phone either. All I can do is wait. I think he and I should be alone tonight."

Michelle downed the last drop of Merlot from her glass and sat back on the sofa. Nathan had been gone for over three hours. She racked her brains trying to think where he could possibly be. Maybe he was in the Meadows. She'd heard that a lot of the youngsters had started sneaking down there at night. They drank and smoked and listened to music. Apparently it was like a mini-Glastonbury at weekends. Michelle shuddered at the thought of the virus meandering among the drunken hugs and kisses, hopping on to shared beer cans and spliffs, then accompanying the kids home and introducing itself to the elderly and vulnerable, family members she'd meet gasping for breath on the wards in a few weeks' time.

She stared down at the rug at her feet. She and Rob had bought it together at Levenshulme Market when they'd first moved into the house. It had a sixties vibe with intersecting electric-blue and vivid yellow squares mixed with silver-grey rectangles and pink circles. While she'd loved its vibrancy and heady mix of colours, Rob said looking at it made him feel like he was on acid. He'd pointed out another in plain blue but, for once, she'd stood her ground. As they were folding it into the boot of their battered Corsa, he'd kissed the top of her head, and said, "You always get your own way." Smiling like a grateful child, she'd kissed him back. The truth was, she'd rarely got her own way in the entirety of their marriage.

Sitting up, she refilled her wine glass from the bottle she'd placed on the bookshelf. As she put it back, she spotted Rob's Man City scarf folded between a pile of Nathan's old Marvel comic books and a couple of her romance novels. The scarf he left behind when he and Nathan had gone to the match at Christmas. They'd bickered bitterly that day. Picking it up , she buried her face in it, thinking about the night they met.

She was supposed to be meeting her friend Jessica at a house party in Fallowfield. Swot that she was, Michelle had been so immersed in her studies that she hadn't noticed the time. She arrived an hour late and the party was already in full rave mode at the rambling Victorian terrace. It was the height of the Madchester rave scene. A DJ in a silver hat and sunglasses was jabbing his fingers in the air on a makeshift podium under a huge chandelier and sweaty students in baggy jeans and T-shirts emblazoned with smiley faces danced frantically to the Happy Mondays. Michelle had never 'dug' the Madchester rave scene – she was a self- confessed nerd with a love of Rush, Def Leopard, and all things prog rock. In her T-shirt, eighties jeans, and John Lennon specs, she was as far removed from the second Summer of Love as you could possibly be. Feeling like a weed in a field of sunflowers, she went from room to room looking for Jessica, who was nowhere to be found.

As she was about to leave, she glanced into the kitchen one last time and was drawn to a Springsteen T-shirt by the sink. Intrigued, she stepped inside. Declaring your love for The Boss at a party like this was a brave, if not foolhardy act. The wearer of the T-shirt was tall and imposing, with a slightly crooked nose and deep-set blue eyes. He was ginger, like her, perhaps strawberry-blonde in a flattering light. As he poured Merrydown Cider into a pint glass, he shouted out something to his friend in a broad Yorkshire accent. She thought of her empty room back at halls.

Taking a deep breath, she stepped towards him, held out a plastic cup, and asked, "What's the best track on the *Born to Run* album?"

After copious amounts of cider and vodka, and an agreement that Thunder Road was by far the superior track, she found herself huddled next to Rob at the foot of the large oak in the garden at three in the morning. She already knew a lot about him at that point: he'd grown up on a farm on the Yorkshire Dales but hated the countryside, he was worried he was heading for a third in his Economics degree because he'd done nothing but party for three years and, as a Young Conservative, he feared John Major might lose the party the next election. He asked her very little about herself. She didn't mind, though. He made her laugh, and his Yorkshire vowel sounds made her feel warm and fuzzy. A plate moon hung high in the clear night sky as he removed her glasses, told her she looked smashing without them, and kissed her. She was nineteen and had never been kissed before.

Michelle stored Rob's scarf away in the cupboard below the bookshelf to keep for Nathan. One marriage, one son, and twenty-eight years later, she and Rob couldn't bear to be in the same room as each other. Yet, she'd loved him once. She pictured his last hours. She'd seen enough to know he'd have had a horrible death. She hoped to God they'd managed to make him comfortable at the end.

Her phone was now buzzing with consoling texts from old friends and members of Rob's family she hadn't seen in years. Clueless about how an embittered ex-wife was supposed to reply, she turned off the phone, curled up on the sofa and drank more wine instead. In the garden an eerie pale-yellow light hovered over the damp grass, making it glisten like yellow gold. As the minutes ticked by, memories of her life with Rob began to surface, like dolphins in the sea of her thoughts.

Half an hour or so later, she was startled by the sound of the side gate slamming. Jumping up, she looked out of the window. Nathan was standing on the patio. The earlier yellow light was now a sepia mist that curled around him. His hoodie up, his chin on his chest, he was gripping one of the patio chairs, as if trying to steady himself. She was immediately reminded her of the day she and Rob had told him they were splitting up, when he'd smashed her beautiful bird table to pieces. Feeling helpless, she waited for another onslaught. Then, as if he sensed she was watching, he looked up. His hands slipping from the chair, he crumpled to his knees on the wet ground, and she went to him.

Anne

"Cheerful reading." Anne perched on the edge of Meg's bed and gestured at the copy of Camus's *The Plague* on the bedside cabinet.

"Cheerful life." Meg scrolled on her phone.

Anne handed her the smoothie she brought her every morning before the start of her online lectures. While most people had found solace in food in lockdown, Meg had lost interest. The healthy organic diet she'd enjoyed so much had been abandoned, and she was losing weight. Her skin stretched over her bony arms and legs, shadows edged her cheekbones, and her loose Blondie T-shirt buried her tiny frame like a billowing sail around a flagpole. It was her eyes that betrayed her declining mental health the most, though. Large and luminous, they filled her gaunt face like two full moons, looking out in terror at a world that had suddenly turned upside-down.

It was six weeks into lockdown and Meg hadn't left the house once. She refused to accompany her or Hakim on their daily walks, or to Morrisons for the weekly shop. They couldn't even tempt her with an outing to the organic food cooperative that she loved so much. Her daily yoga was a thing of the past, and she'd recently started going back to bed after her morning lectures and napping until four or five in the afternoon. Anne calculated that she was sleeping thirteen or fourteen hours a day. It was a death-like slumber, and it was hard to shake her out of it. It reminded Anne of the days when her father was floored by his 'black dog'. She and Hannah, small and energetic little girls at the time, would bound into his room and hurl themselves on his bed in the morning. Growling, he'd send them away, desperate to slip back into the hibernation he preferred to the waking hours he seemed to find so torturous.

Meg took the smoothie, placed it on her bedside cabinet, and grabbed the small bottle of sanitizer that she always kept within reach. After cleansing her hands, she passed the bottle to Anne. Anne noticed the inflamed, chapped skin on Meg's pencil-thin fingers. Meg washed her hands twenty or more times a day, scrubbing for a long time. Though Anne had already washed her hands five minutes before, she did it again, dreading the argument that would follow if she didn't. Meg's hand-cleanliness didn't extend to her room. There was no logic to any of it. Damp towels hung on chairs, clothes were scattered all over the floor, and make-up, toiletries, and dirty plates were piled on every surface. It was hardly what you'd expect from someone who'd done a sterling job of living independently for six months. Anne was fed up of cleaning up after her and was now refusing to do it anymore.

Meg lifted the smoothie to her lips.

"Strawberries and blackberries – your favourite," said Anne.

"You did wash them thoroughly, didn't you, Mummy?"

"Of course."

Meg sipped. "Yummy." She nodded down at her phone. "Seventy-six thousand new cases yesterday. And four hundred and thirteen deaths."

Anne sighed. "Fixating on the numbers won't do you any good, darling."

"Easier said than done, Mummy. Easier said than done." Meg sipped again. "I don't feel very well this morning. Would you mind soothing my noggin for a bit before class?"

Anne felt a tug on her heart. "Of course."

In Meg's dark period, when her anxiety fizzed and bubbled her brain and prevented her from going to school, she would often search Anne out and ask her for a head massage. Meg would sit on cushions on the floor in front of the TV and Anne would knead her tiny shoulders, neck, and various points on her head. Meg said the rhythm calmed her spiralling thoughts. She said she understood why dogs and cats liked to be stroked so much. 'Soothing the noggin' they'd named it, and Anne would often do it until her arms ached.

Meg positioned herself on a chair and Anne stood behind her. "Heard anything more from Josh?" she asked, starting on Meg's bony shoulders. A few days before, she had told her she'd ended the relationship.

"He keeps texting, but I'm not replying. It's over. End of."

"Did anything happen between you?"

"Nothing, apart from the realisation that he's as dull as fuck. God. Those awful orange trousers."

Anne laughed. "They were quite something, weren't they? Keep your head still. I'm sure you'll meet someone else more exciting."

"How? In case you hadn't heard, Mummy, we're not allowed to meet other humans, and I'm not really a cyber-sex kind of girl."

"Everything will be back to normal soon. You'll see." Anne stopped kneading and flexed her arm, taken aback by how unconvincing she sounded.

"And then what? Another terrorist attack or climate-change disaster? Or maybe a good old-fashioned war?"

"The vaccine will be here any day now."

"No way am I being injected with some crap Big Pharma have rushed through in a couple of months."

"Try to think of the positives, darling," Anne said through gritted teeth.

She could really do without one of Meg's meltdowns right now. She was still reeling after the bombshell Hannah had delivered two days before. She had barely slept since.

Meg suddenly pushed her hands away, and turned round, her eyes blazing. "Think of the positives? I don't know if you remember but, when I was fifteen, I couldn't even get through the school gates because I was suffering from an anxiety disorder. Then, at seventeen, I went to a concert, and a psycho planted a bomb and killed twenty-two kids my age. And now, just when I finally find a bit of peace at uni, a global pandemic forces me to live back here with you and Dad like I'm a freakin' toddler again! And don't even get me started on climate change!"

Anne opened her mouth to speak, but Meg put her forefinger on her lips.

"I'm not done. The online education you and Dad are shelling out for is a pile of crap, and the uni is robbing us for rent when we aren't even staying there. Think of the positives? Why don't you ask Nathan to think of the positives? His dad just died of Covid, and he can't even go to the funeral. Seriously, Mother! Next thing, you'll be telling me these are the best years of my life!"

Anne was rescued by the dial tone for the start of Meg's online lessons. Like the alarm waking passengers on a cruise ship, the sound spread through the house every morning. Anne made a quick exit and headed downstairs. It was the only sensible thing to do when Meg was like this. She could be so wretched at times. Anne had to constantly remind herself that she wasn't well and couldn't help her meltdowns.

Hakim was heading out for his morning walk before he started work in the spare bedroom. She took out some cleaning products from under the sink and started on the kitchen. She attacked the worktop with vigour, and rubbed the back of her neck. She was full of tension. She wouldn't mind a massage herself.

Anne had spoken to Michelle a few times since Rob's death. She said Nathan was struggling. Anne had no idea Meg was in contact with him again, but what could she do about it?

As she worked she reflected on what Meg had just said. Her words resonated. In the past few years, the world *had* been in a permanent crisis, and young people *had* suffered disproportionately through no fault of their own. As they set off on their journey to adulthood, world events had buffeted them like sailors navigating a rough sea. And yet, while Anne had no doubt that some of these crises and external events had contributed to Meg's mental-health issues, she also strongly suspected that she had probably inherited a predisposition for depression and anxiety from her grandfather. It was all terribly unfair, and there was no magic cure for any of it. It was something Meg would have to learn to navigate and manage throughout her life. Neither she nor Hakim could fix it either. That was tough. What parent ever stops searching for a solution for their child's problems? Wasn't it every mother or father's mission to make sure they were happy?

Anne started to wipe down the kitchen cabinets, tears suddenly springing to her eyes as she remembered her conversation with Hannah the previous evening.

When Anne found Jimmy McGreevy's obituary in the Irish newspaper, she reread it several times. Pausing at the sentence that mentioned his involvement in the murder of military personnel in London, she mulled over dates and was suddenly compelled to discover if he was any way connected to her father's death. Yet it all seemed too much of a wild coincidence – Michelle was one of her best friends and McGreevy was her uncle, for God's sake! Could he really have been involved?

As a colonel in the army, her father had completed a number of tours of duty in Northern Ireland. When he was killed, the IRA had been conducting a concerted bombing campaign over here, making them the obvious suspects for his murder. The despicable vermin who'd planted the bomb under his car had never been found and brought to justice, something that always puzzled Anne as she grew older. She was only fourteen when he died, Hannah seventeen. They were too young and traumatised to pursue the case themselves, but her father had influential friends in high places in the army and the Met Police. Why had they and her mother given up so easily? Anne had read about other families who had lost loved ones in the Troubles, who fought tirelessly for years to find their killers. Why not her father?

His death had left Anne floundering, without a buoy or anchor. She'd desperately wanted answers, but her mother always shut her down whenever she broached the subject.

"There's no point," she'd snap. "It's never going to bring him back. Better leave well alone."

When she googled Jimmy McGreevy, her online search yielded little. A couple of tabloid articles reported his trial and subsequent sentencing for placing a bomb in a bin outside a London store, but there was nothing specific about his involvement in the bombing of military personnel. She needed to delve further. It was pointless asking her mother. These days, she could hardly remember her own name. Hannah might know something, though, so Anne took some screen shots of the obituary and the tabloid articles she'd found and emailed them to her sister.

Minutes later, Hannah rang back.

Not wanting Hakim or Meg to overhear the conversation, Anne slipped into the garden. It was a warm night, and she sat down at the table under an angry blistering pink sky,

"Did you read the bit about military personnel?" Anne asked excitedly.

"Yes."

"So?"

"What?"

"Don't you think McGreevy could have been a suspect in Daddy's murder?"

Hannah let out a long sigh. "Oh, Annie darling. You've got it all wrong. Look at the dates. This McGreevy chap couldn't have been involved. He was arrested without bail a couple of months before Daddy died. He would have been in the clink at the time."

Anne brought up the screenshots on her phone and read again, her heart dropping. "Yes, you're right. But even if he didn't plant the bomb itself, he could still have been involved, couldn't he?"

A short silence followed, then Hannah cleared her throat. "Look, sis, there's something important I need to tell you. It's about Daddy."

Eileen

Eileen knocked on the window at the back of Michelle's house and waited. When Michelle didn't come, she knocked a second time.

Nathan slid open the door. "She's in the shower," he said sullenly.

Unshaven, in a Blossoms T-shirt, flip-flops and shorts, he looked wild-eyed and sleep-deprived.

"OK. I'll wait."

As he retreated inside, she called after him. "So sorry to hear about your dad!"

He turned slowly and gave her an icy stare. "You're not one bit sorry. You hated him. You always made that pretty clear, Eileen."

Wounded, she stepped backwards as he disappeared into the house. Michelle had told her that he was taking Rob's death very badly, with mood swings and aggression directed at her. Poor Nathan. He'd had never been her favourite person, but nobody deserved to lose a father at his age.

She sat down at the garden table. It was a dull June day, neither too hot, nor too cold. She looked up at a huge cauliflower-shaped cloud drifting across the white-grey sky. Alex would be up there now, halfway across the Atlantic on his flight home.

Michelle emerged a few minutes later in her scrubs, carrying two mugs of coffee. Her hair was damp and she looked tired but, after weeks of illness, the colour was finally returning to her cheeks. She handed Eileen a mug. Then, even though she'd already had the virus, she sat at the far end of the table out of habit.

"You look so much better," said Eileen.

"I feel less corpse-like but I'm not a hundred percent yet."

"I don't understand how Sergio and I have escaped the virus, especially with him working at the deli." Eileen sipped her coffee. "So, how did the funeral go?" she asked tentatively.

"The video link didn't work so we had to hear about it in a phone call from Jane."

"Oh, no!"

"I could kill her, the way she went ahead with it without Nathan being able to get there. It was a logistical nightmare and, as much as we tried, we couldn't get him on a plane on time. He was gutted. A lot of Rob and Jane's friends are retired ex-pats, too terrified to leave their homes, so in the end only three people attended: Jane and Terry and Chris, a gay couple from Stockport who owned the villa next door."

"God!"

"Jane draped the coffin in a Man City banner as Nathan had requested – at least she let him have that, then the three of them accompanied him to the crematorium for a ten-minute service. Jane read a poem and they played Springsteen's 'The River', and Deep Purple's 'Smoke on the Water'. When I told Nathan he cried his eyes out then stomped upstairs to his room and played both songs at full volume for hours."

Eileen shook her head slowly. "That's just heart-breaking."

"It'll take him a long time to get over it." Michelle sighed. "Anyway, do you mind if we talk about something else. How's Alex?"

"Currently on an American Airlines flight on his way home."

Michelle spluttered her coffee. "*What?*"

"I didn't tell you as you've had so much going on these past few days, but he's had to leave New York."

"No! Why?"

"He got arrested on one of the Black Lives Matter protests. He was advised to leave before he got deported."

"Never!"

"It's been a turbulent few days."

Michelle stared at her, open-mouthed. "What exactly happened?"

Eileen sat back, a ray of sun warming her face. "He'd already been on a number of peaceful protests with his boyfriend Ross and Madison, including one in front of Trump Towers. Then three days ago, he facetimed me and told me that he and Madison were going on another march that evening on their own. Apparently, Ross was working. I told him to be careful, as I always did. The next morning, I got a call from Shannon. She told me that Alex and Madison had been arrested. Apparently, the pair of eejits were violating some kind of eight o'clock curfew and they got caught up in an incident on the Brooklyn Bridge. When I spoke to Alex he told me the police charged and kettled them. He and Madison started running away but a cop caught a hold of Madison. When Alex ran back and tried to help her, they were both put in a van for resisting arrest and taken to a police precinct."

"Bloody hell!"

"He said all the noise and commotion triggered memories of the Arena. He said when he ran back to get Madison, he panicked and probably overreacted towards the police.

"Really?"

"Anyway, remember I told you I met a cousin when I was over there who's in NYPD?

"The Trump supporter?"

"Yes. Martin. Shannon asked him for help. He knew some of the cops on duty in the precinct that night. He managed to pull a few strings and they let them out."

"It's like an episode of *NYPD Blue*."

"Isn't it? Shannon said that US immigration is really strict about any kind of misdemeanours and resisting arrest could have been classed as aggravated felony. Alex was only on a temporary and was in danger of being deported."

Michelle frowned. "And if he got deported, he'd never be allowed back in the States again."

"Exactly. According to Martin, it probably wouldn't happen, but his advice was not to take the risk and to get on a flight home ASAP."

"Poor Alex. That's so unfair."

"I know but he did a very stupid thing, Michelle. He didn't stop to think about his situation."

"How is he taking it?"

"He's devastated, especially about leaving Ross behind."

They both watched a grey squirrel dart across the lawn in front of them and run up the garden fence.

"Jesus," said Michelle. "Nathan's lost his dad, Meg's mental health has gone down the pan again, and now Alex has had to leave

New York." She shook her head. "The pandemic is claiming a lot more victims than just those of us getting the virus."

Alex's plane had landed. Eileen made her way from the multistorey car park to the designated pick-up point outside the arrivals building. The airport was eerily quiet. On a June evening in normal times, it would have been bursting with noise: the buzz of travellers' excited conversation, the bump and roll of suitcase wheels, the roar of planes overhead. Now it was as silent and empty as the skies above. Signs for a new Covid testing site were everywhere and she had glimpsed a huge white tent and a few health workers in scrubs and masks. On a runway, she counted ten EasyJet planes parked in line, like a row of dead birds with clipped, orange-tipped wings.

A small crowd had gathered outside the arrivals building. Through the window, she could see a couple of security guards hovering by the shuttered shops, a cleaner pushing a cart, and a lonely cabin crew member wheeling an overnight case behind single masked travellers. Nearby, a girl of five or six stood next to her mother, jumping from foot to foot, and holding up a sign saying, "*Welcome home, Daddy*".

Eileen sat down on one of the metal chairs not marked with an X, took a sip from her water bottle, and waited. She imagined how Alex must have felt as his plane touched down onto the Manchester tarmac. Regretful, angry, hard done by. But above all, he must be feeling a huge sense of loss for the life he'd abruptly had to leave behind. She certainly wasn't expecting a joyous reunion scene.

When he finally emerged through the revolving doors, she ran to him and hugged him tightly. Though she shared his pain, relief flooded out of her to have him home safe. As they walked back to the car park, she stole glances at him out of the corner of her eye. Hunched forwards, he seemed weighed down by so much more than his rucksack. Two new frown lines had furrowed into his brow, like an equals sign. The word crestfallen came to mind, a term she often taught her students in creative writing lessons. It derived from the image of a horse with its crest (head) on its chest after defeat in a battle. That was exactly how Alex appeared now.

She rambled on, filling the silent void. "Dad can't wait to see you. He got up early to make your favourite chorizo and bean stew. The pubs and restaurants are opening soon, and Boris said we can go on staycations. We could go to Anglesey for a few days. Did I tell you we've accepted an offer on the house here? Oh, and Grandad says the builders are starting back on the Mayo house next week."

He muttered something in reply, but his words were swallowed up by the sound of a plane taking off nearby. Unused to the sight and sound, they both looked up in surprise.

They walked on, and when she started babbling again Alex slowed down. "Stop it, Mum!" he snapped. "I know you're trying to cheer me up but I have zero interest in pubs and restaurants opening, or trips to Anglesey, or the house in Mayo for that matter. I don't give two fucks about any of it, *because I don't want to be here. OK?*"

On the drive home he pretended to be asleep. He looked deeply unhappy. Who wouldn't be, in his shoes? He'd made one stupid mistake and he'd lost everything.

CHAPTER 18

Michelle

Seeing Billy again stirred Michelle deeply. She had just parked in Chorlton Precinct car park when she saw him loading bags of groceries into the boot of his car nearby. Clean-shaven and tanned, he looked like he'd put on weight. She winced when she saw he was wearing the Ted Baker shirt she'd got him early on in their relationship. She'd bought it on a whim in the Trafford Centre, because it matched the cobalt-blue of his eyes.

"Sure, it's not even my birthday," he'd said, lifting it out of the bag.

He'd seemed embarrassed by her extravagance, and she'd been mortified. The memory triggered that same feeling now. How could she have been so stupid and needy? She tried to remember if he'd ever given her a gift during their time together. She couldn't remember one.

She'd come out in a sweatshirt and jeans without make-up and her hair was frizzing in all directions. She looked around for an escape route, but Billy had already spotted her. When he raised a hand in a wave, she reluctantly headed towards him. Meeting him again might have been easier if he'd looked like the grubby alcoholic he was when she'd last seen him but, as she neared, she saw he was back to his rugged, handsome self. He shut the car boot and, when he turned to look at her, her heart did a somersault.

"How's it going?" he asked with a tentative smile.

"Hello, Billy." Her face burning, she fumbled with her phone, trying but failing to slip it casually into the side pocket of her bag.

When she looked up, the expression on his face was akin to the look you give a small child who has fallen over and needs help to get to their feet. She didn't want his pity and in that moment she hated herself.

He leaned back against the car and folded his arms across his chest. "So how have you been in these crazy times?"

"Fabulous. Just fabulous."

"I often thought of you working away at the hospital saving lives," he said gently. "It must have been hell."

"Oh, stop it. You'll be clapping next." She shrugged. "I went to work every day. A lot of people did."

He shifted on the car uncomfortably. "At least we're coming out of it now though, eh?"

"I wouldn't be too sure about that."

"You reckon?"

"Not until there's a vaccine rollout. There could be a second wave any time."

He pulled a face of mock horror. "Ah, now, don't say that."

She cleared her throat. "You look well, Billy."

"Thank you." He smiled, the corners of his eyes crinkling, and her heart melted. "Your beady eye has probably noticed that I'm off the drink."

She nodded. "It has been noted. That's great news."

"Sure what was the alternative? Being locked in twenty-four-seven with the kids and drinking myself into a stupor?"

"It can't have been easy. Well done." She gestured over to the ticket machine. "Anyway, I'd better go and get a ticket, or I'll get fined."

She started to walk away.

"Look after yourself!" he called after her, in a voice not void of tenderness.

Michelle's hand shook as she inserted coins into the machine and took her ticket. She exited the car park feeling disconcerted, the old Buzzcocks' song, "Ever Fallen in Love" (with someone you shouldn't have fallen in love with) filling her head. Her brother Tommy used to play it all the time in his bedroom when he was going through his punk phase. Drunk on pool-sized glasses of Merlot, she too had played it on a loop in the days after she and Billy split. Making her way to the High Street, she tried her best to purge all thoughts of him from her mind.

Now that non-essential shops had re-opened, Michelle was on the hunt for a fiftieth birthday present for Amir. After weeks on the

Covid ward, he had finally been allowed home weeks ago in early May. The staff on duty that day, his friends and colleagues, and a Channel 4 camera crew had all lined up along the corridor to give him a celebrity exit. Michelle had escaped her ward round for a few minutes to cheer him on.

That evening, she spotted herself on the six o'clock news, waving and clapping in the background.

Amir had called her not long afterwards. "That was so embarrassing, McGreevy," he'd said, laughing. "I was certainly not my handsome best."

His youngest, Nadia, had moved into his flat in Didsbury to look after him. Michelle had visited a few times. He seemed to have returned to his cheeky, nerdy old self again, but she sensed an underbelly of deep sadness, a shadow beneath the laughter and smiles. She recognised it because she had it too. They joked about his brush with death and got competitive about their Covid symptoms. Amir won hands down. Apart from a few muscle aches, she was more or less back to normal. He, on the other hand, was permanently exhausted, could just about walk around unaided, and was undergoing tests for scarring on his lungs. Despite all this, he'd agreed to a small birthday barbeque in his garden, after the recent government announcement that gatherings of thirty or more were now permitted.

Michelle went from shop to shop looking for a gift. After careful consideration, she decided on a signed copy of Kamila Shamsie's latest novel because she'd seen him reading her last one, a selection of cheeses because his taste and smell had returned, and a bottle of single malt because he liked a tipple.

Walking back to the car park, she smiled down at the bag of grandiose gifts by her side. She recalled the days when the pair of them were skint students counting out their small change to see if they could stretch to one bottle of Merrydown Cider or two. They were naïve twenty-somethings at the time. How could they have ever imagined that they'd both be struck down by a mystery virus in a global pandemic?

Nathan was out when she got home, which was unusual as he usually slept in until one or two in the afternoon. Since Rob's death, he'd become practically nocturnal. He disappeared in the evenings, returned at all hours, then slept for most of the day. Michelle tried her best to talk to him about how he was feeling, but he volunteered very little. He seemed to have lost contact with his friends too. She no longer heard him chatting to them on the Xbox, or on his phone, the way he used to. She hadn't seen him open a medical textbook or do any academic work on his laptop for ages either.

"Now that things are opening up, why don't you get yourself a little job?" she said, over dinner the other day. "They're looking for staff everywhere. It might stop you dwelling on things."

He laughed sarcastically. "Stop me dwelling on things? My dad just died. Of course I'm going to fuckin' well dwell on it."

"That's not what I meant."

He threw her a murderous look. "If you'd never got divorced, Dad would be sitting at the table with us now. How about you dwell on that?"

Throwing down his fork, he left the room. She sat with her head in her hands, feeling the punch of his blame yet again. She no longer knew what to do or say around him. His moods changed like the wind, and it was hard to see his heart-wrenching sadness. He had truly adored Rob. He was angry at her a lot of the time, and she sometimes got the impression that he thought the wrong parent had died. And she understood his anger. He'd felt repeatedly abandoned by the father he idolized – first after the divorce, then when Rob moved to Spain, and now permanently in death.

She put Amir's presents away in a kitchen cupboard and cleaned up some of Nathan's mess. Where could he possibly be disappearing to every night? Recently she'd begun to wonder if his grief had turned him to drugs. She'd always known he smoked weed and dabbled in other things, but had his anger propelled him to the hard stuff? Overcome by panic, she suddenly decided to search his room.

She went through trouser pockets, backpacks and drawers. She looked under the bed, lifted his mattress, and swiped every shelf. His desk was complete chaos, and she emptied boxes of pens and pulled out books and sheets of paper. She found no drugs, but she did find a letter in an envelope, with a university stamp on it. She hesitated. Nathan was a grown adult. She shouldn't be reading his mail. Stuff that, she told herself. These were exceptional times. She pulled out the letter and read.

RE: Termination of Studies at The School of Medicine, University of Liverpool.

Dear Nathan,

I hope this letter finds you well. I am writing to inform you of a decision that has been made regarding your academic standing at the University of Liverpool. After careful consideration, I regret to tell you that your studies at our institution have been terminated.

This decision follows a thorough review of your academic performance and conduct. The decision was not an easy one to make but I would like to clarify the reasons that have led to this outcome:

1. **Academic Performance: Your academic performance has consistently fallen below the minimum standards required for satisfactory progress in your chosen programme. Despite our efforts to provide you with support and opportunities for improvement, your grades and coursework have not shown significant signs of improvement.**

2. **Academic Misconduct: Regrettably, we have identified two instances of academic misconduct during your time at the university. Both involved**

cheating in exams. These actions violate the university's academic integrity policies, which are fundamental to the principles of fairness, honesty, and trust in academia.

3. Failure to Meet Academic Milestones: You have also failed to meet the academic milestones and requirements set forth in your programme's curriculum. This includes incomplete coursework, missed deadlines, and failure to complete required projects or assessments.

We understand that the recent the global pandemic may have played a role in your academic struggles. However, despite efforts made to provide you with support, your academic performance and behaviour have not shown sufficient improvement to continue your studies.

Please be advised that you have the right to appeal this decision. If you wish to do so, please refer to the university's appeals process.

We wish you the best in the future. Should you have any questions or require further clarification regarding this decision, please do not hesitate to contact me or the Office of the Dean of Studies.

Yours sincerely,

Jennifer Raddings

Dean of Studies, School of Medicine

University of Liverpool

Michelle slumped down onto the bed, feeling like she'd been winded. She turned the envelope over to check the postage date. The letter had been sent weeks ago, and Nathan hadn't said a word about it to her.

Anne

"Not for me." Hakim put his hand over his wine glass. "We really need to cut down, darling. Lockdown has turned us into raving alcoholics."

"Oh, don't be such a bore," said Anne, filling her glass to the brim. "Well, I'm jolly well filling my boots after the week I've had."

She placed the bottle back on the coffee table.

Hakim rubbed her leg. "I do think Hannah would have told you about your father sooner or later, you know."

"Really?" She gulped from her glass and frowned. "I don't."

She sat back on the sofa, picked up the remote and started to browse Netflix. "Let's have a comedy," she said. "I can't bear any more misery. No psychological thrillers about missing children or murdered wives. No police dramas either. The sight of forensic police in hazmat suits makes me think of Covid and gives me the heebie-jeebies."

Despite Hakim's protests that it looked a bit girly, they settled on *Bridesmaids*, a US comedy that Eileen had recommended. Kirsten Wiig and John Hamm were getting it on in a raunchy bedroom scene when they heard Meg's footsteps coming down the stairs. A few seconds later, she popped her head around the door.

Anne paused the film with the remote and sat up. "Darling, you look fabulous!" she exclaimed.

For the first time in ages, Meg was wearing make-up. Her cheeks were blushed, she had teal-green glitter on her eyelids that matched her Fair-Trade hoodie, and gloss glistened on her lips. She'd also washed and straightened her hair, and a colourful cloth mask nestled under her chin.

"Going for a walk with a friend," she said breezily, before disappearing out of the front door.

Hakim turned to Anne open-mouthed. "Holy cow! She's not left the house in three months. I wonder who she's meeting?"

Anne pressed play on the remote. She had her suspicions about whom Meg was meeting but, if she voiced them, Hakim would be chasing her down the street like a foxhound.

Recently, Meg had let slip that she was talking to Nathan quite often on Snapchat or WhatsApp, or whatever platform it was they used. She said she was helping him talk through stuff after Rob's death. While Anne understood that the boy must be going through hell, if she was completely honest she still didn't want Meg anywhere near him. The mere thought of Meg meeting Nathan in the flesh made her reach for her wine. At the moment Meg was fragile. Nathan could easily lead her down the destructive path of drink and drugs and into an unhealthy relationship again. Anne sighed. If they did get back together, there wasn't a thing she could do about it. Meg was a grown adult. She had no control over whom she dated.

Hakim was soon laughing out loud at the film but, as much as she tried, Anne couldn't concentrate. Her thoughts kept meandering back to the phone conversation with Hannah in the garden.

Anne had been disappointed when Hannah told her that Jimmy McGreevy couldn't have been involved in Daddy's murder. It was a long shot, but for a short while she'd dared to hope that she might finally be able to get some closure over his death.

Then Hannah told her truth about what had actually happened.

"At the time of Daddy's death, the IRA were targeting lots of military personnel and politicians over here," she said. "Daddy was trained to check underneath his car for bombs. He did it religiously. Don't you remember?"

"Not really."

"Didn't you think it strange how we never all got into the car together? He always made you and me and Mummy wait in the house until he gave us the all-clear., then he'd give us the all-clear."

"So?"

"Oh, Annie darling. He checked for a bomb that morning too. Mummy was looking out of the window, and she saw him." Her voice faltered. "But he opened the car door anyway."

Anne inhaled sharply. Her mind struggled to grasp what Hannah had said.

"Annie?"

"You mean he ..."

"He killed himself. Yes. He'd been clinically depressed for so long. He simply couldn't take it anymore. That's why nobody ever searched for his killers. Mummy told them not to. She told me everything a few weeks after it happened."

Anne's mobile slackened in her grip as she searched for the right words to say.

"Annie, sweetie. Are you there?"

"You never told me."

"We did it to protect you. You were only fourteen, and you worshipped the ground he walked on. Mummy didn't want to tell anyone. She was ashamed. Suicide was a terrible taboo back then."

"But afterwards ... all those years ... didn't you ever think I had a right to know?"

"I did actually, but whenever I broached the subject with Mummy, she was adamant. She didn't want to dredge it all up again." Hannah was crying now. "I'm so sorry, Annie. We genuinely thought it was best that you didn't know."

When the call was over, Anne placed the phone on the table and stared down at the rotting tree stump beside her. It had once been a beautiful silver birch, with a plume of branches stretching the entire width of the narrow garden, and a slender trunk that shone like metal. A young tree, it had got sick with birch dieback, so they'd had to have it felled. She'd been taken aback at how distraught she'd felt watching it drop to the ground before its time.

Numb with shock, she rose from her chair and began pacing the garden, trying to process what Hannah had told her. Things started to make sense: the way Mummy had eliminated all trace of Daddy from the house after he died, the lack of interest in pursuing the case, and her recent ramblings. "How could he have abandoned us like that?" she had repeated over and over.

Anne suddenly stopped pacing and steadied herself against the garden fence. A memory came to her from the days after Daddy's death, something she must have buried, that now emerged in her mind like a shooting star illuminating the darkness of that terrible time.

Paparazzi swarmed outside the house, cameras flashing intermittently, while inside every room was packed to the rafters with a flurry of important, busy-looking men: detectives, forensic police, Daddy's army colleagues, and members of M16, all talking in hushed tones. They'd set up a base in the kitchen, with additional phones and boxes of files.

Anne had felt a stab of anger when she'd spotted one of them casually helping himself to Daddy's whisky from the decanter in the dining room. Despite being ordered to stay in their rooms, she and Hannah huddled at the top of the staircase, silently watching the comings and goings. Anne told herself that if they all went away Daddy would walk through the door again.

At some point, the dining-room door opened and Daddy's good friend, Colonel McKenna, came out. He was dabbing his eyes with a large handkerchief. Behind him, Mummy was sitting at the long oak table, her face buried in her hands. She and Hannah watched as Colonel McKenna gathered all the men together in the living room and shut the door behind them. Shortly afterwards, they all packed up their things and left. Anne was now certain that that was the moment Mummy made the call. He had committed suicide, she had decided, and she didn't want his death investigated as a murder.

It had started to rain and Anne stepped away from the garden fence, fighting back tears as she imagined the utter despair her father must have felt when he made that split-second decision to open the car door. It was an opportunity to end his life, without it looking like suicide – he could spare his family the pain of discovering he no longer wanted to be in the world with them. If Mummy hadn't been looking out of the window and seen him, none of them would have been any the wiser.

Anne also felt angry. She and Hannah were young girls. How could he have abandoned them like that? Poor embittered Mummy. To have witnessed him die such a violent death, and never to have spoken about it for all those years must have been an unspeakable burden.

Anne had always viewed her mother as cold and heartless, an unapproachable figure wrapped up in emotional barbed wire. Only now did she understand that she had shut all her feelings down as a coping mechanism.

Daddy had taken his own life, but someone had planted that bomb to enable him to do it. The more she thought about it, the more she was convinced that Mummy should have pursued the case. It was too late now, though. Terrorists like Jimmy McGreevy were either dead or had been released from jail as part of the Peace Agreement. She would never know who placed the bomb under the car, and the not knowing would always haunt her.

Anne went back to the table to fetch her phone. It was raining heavily. Meg would get drenched on her walk. As she picked up the phone, she realised she must have left the ringer off when she saw two missed calls from Meg, and a text that read: **"Ring me back Mummy NOW. Something terrible has happened."**

Eileen

Eileen could smell burning. Sergio had flopped onto the bed fully clothed and woken her. He reeked of dope. Flinging off the duvet, she followed the burning smell into the box room where she found a spliff smouldering on the edge of the overflowing ashtray. Cursing, she stubbed it out. One of these days the fecking gobshite would burn the house down with all of them in it.

Sergio's laptop was still open, and he hadn't signed out. Without hesitating or knowing why, she closed the door behind her, sat down, and clicked open his email account. The inbox was full of the usual unsolicited crap, notifications from social media, people selling stuff, and music-streaming notifications and Ticketmaster alerts. There was hardly any personal correspondence at all. Apart from one.

Ten minutes later, she found herself on the sofa in the living room with her head in her hands. Spanish phrases swam around her brain. *No, me arrepiento de nada* – No, I don't regret any of it. *Ansio verte* – I long to see you. *Mi cuerpo te quiere* – My body wants you.

Each declaration pierced her heart like gunfire. She'd worked out who the woman was as soon as she read the words "lockdown in Barcelona". It was pretty, dark-haired Carla from Clay Corner who had returned to her home city. Joyous, lovely Carla whom Anne had praised from morning until night. Eileen had met her briefly when she'd dropped in to see Anne one day. They'd joked about why she was living in rainy Manchester when she could be in Barcelona. What was she? Twenty-four or five? Middle-aged, married man fucks someone half his age. Could it be any more of a cliché? When did it start? When Sergio began working at the deli or before? But that was months ago. Eileen remembered the sudden improvement in his mood. She hit her forehead with the palm of her hand. She'd put it down to finding a job. Not finding a young lover. She pictured him fucking Carla's pert body. She looked down at the veins on her hands and her sagging breasts. What twenty-five-year-old would want to fuck her?

How had she not noticed? All those hours spent on his laptop during lockdown. She'd believed him when he said he was reconnecting with family and friends in Spain. Why wouldn't she? Everyone was reconnecting with everyone in lockdown. She sat up on the sofa. *Jesus.* All those days when she was in New York, and she couldn't contact him. He'd made up all kinds of excuses. She glanced around the room and swallowed. Had he fucked her here, in their home?

For years she'd defended him to her family and friends, telling them he was an artist and musician, and excusing him from doing menial jobs. He was depressed, she'd said, he'd get a job when he was feeling better. Other women might have kicked him out years ago, but she'd dug her heels in and continued to build a life around him. She'd done it because she loved him with every bone in her body. And this was how he'd thanked her.

When she eventually stopped sobbing, panic set in and an army of intrusive thoughts started to invade her mind. Was he going to leave her? Was he going to return to Spain and be with Carla? People everywhere were having life-changing moments. Maybe Sergio was too. And what about the house in Mayo? Now she knew why he'd been dragging his heels about it. Thinking she was going mad, she sat back, took deep breaths and told herself to calm down.

She decided not to wake him and confront him now. It was the middle of the night, he was stoned, and she'd get no sense from him at all. Instead, she pulled a throw over herself and curled up on the sofa in a foetal position. A bottle smashed somewhere on the estate as her thoughts continued to circle around her head with nowhere to land. The wall clock said it was just before midnight. Closing her eyes, Eileen waited for a sleep she knew would never come.

Then she heard her phone ringing upstairs.

Michelle

Michelle slipped her mask below her chin and looked out of the hospital window. It was one-thirty in the morning. They must be freezing out there on that bench at this ungodly hour. Visitors still weren't allowed, but Anne and Eileen had come to be with her in her hour of need, and she loved them for that. She walked along the corridor and through the thronging A&E reception area. As the glass doors opened and she stepped out into the cold night air, she hesitated. How could she talk about it? How could she put into words the unspeakable thing that her child, the child they had known since birth, had done? It was too late to go back in now, though. They had already seen her. Pulling her coat tight around her, she went to them.

They held each other in a lengthy embrace, and none of them spoke for a while.

"How is he?" asked Eileen as they pulled away.

"Out of danger." She sat down between them on the bench.

"Thank God," said Anne.

"He's still on a drip. We have to wait and see if there's any liver damage before he can come home."

Michelle had been at work when it happened. Of course she bloody had. An accident on the M6 had kept her busy all evening, and she hadn't seen any of Meg's messages or voice mails until after eleven. Nathan had arranged to meet Meg for a walk in Chorlton Park at eight. When he didn't turn up or respond to any of her messages, she'd started to worry. Soon afterwards he texted her.

"Fucked everything up. Fucked up you, the love of my life. Fucked up uni. Fucked up friends. Miss Dad so much. Tell Mum I'm sorry."

Panicking, Meg hurried to the house. When Nathan didn't answer the door, she recalled the spare key that was kept in the plant pot by the side gate from the time they were together. She let herself in. To find him like that. Lying on his bed, barely conscious, wearing his dad's City scarf, the paracetamol packets and empty whisky bottle on the floor beside him.

It was a quiet night for the emergency services, thank God. Covid callouts were on the decrease, so the ambulance was able to get to him in time and take him to Wythenshawe Hospital. Michelle wasn't sure she could have coped if he'd arrived at her place. Her colleague, Vicky, got out of bed and came in to cover for her so she could go over to Wythenshawe. When she arrived, Nathan was in ICU. Oh, the shock and the brutal, out-of-the-blue bullet of it! Never for a second did she ever think he would attempt to take his own life.

Minutes ago, she'd thought she wouldn't be able to talk about it at all, but, safe with Anne and Eileen, she suddenly felt the need. Soon everything was flooding out of her like water from a cracked pipe.

"He was obviously severely depressed. He'd isolated himself from his friends, he spent hours and hours sleeping, and he was permanently angry. I knew he was struggling after Rob's death, but I tried to get him to talk about it. I really did. Maybe I could have taken time off work to be with him, or I could have pushed him more to get grief-counselling. But what good would that do? Whenever I tried to speak to him he told me to leave him alone. He said he was dealing with it, but he obviously wasn't."

Anne squeezed her shoulders. "None of this is your fault," she said.

"Anne's right. Don't you dare blame yourself, Michelle." Eileen put a hand on her back. "You've been through hell these past months. Going into that hospital every day and deciding who was sick enough to go on a Covid ward and who wasn't, watching your colleagues get seriously ill, and signing death certificate after death certificate. It was more than any mortal could cope with. You've been traumatised."

Anne handed her a tissue as one of the ambulances in front of them moved off silently.

Michelle wiped her nose.

"When he started going out every evening, I thought he was taking drugs, but Meg said he'd been walking for miles, trying to keep the thoughts of harming himself at bay. She told me there was something happening online with him too. I haven't got to the bottom of that yet." She looked at Anne. "I owe Meg his life. Apparently they've been talking for months about how low he's been feeling."

Anne took her hand. "If I remember correctly, Nathan saved Meg's life once too."

Later, as she walked back to the ward, Michelle felt a surge of anger. *How could you do this to me?* she wanted to yell at him, *I gave birth to you in this hospital, I gave you life, and I nurtured you for twenty years. How could you want to throw it all away?*

By the time she entered the ward, the rage had dissolved, and she felt ashamed of herself. Nathan was a sick boy and he needed help. She tiptoed in behind the closed curtain and slipped into the chair beside his bed. He was sleeping soundly. Leaning forward, she gingerly removed a lock of hair that had flopped down over his eyes. It felt silky between her finger and thumb.

"My beautiful boy," she whispered, laying her head face down on the bed beside him.

PART SIX

CHAPTER 19

Nine months later

April 2021

Eileen

Spring was in full throttle in the Meadows. Carpets of bluebells and cherry blossom dazzled, robins serenaded each other, and clusters of hawthorn were starting to appear, like shy girls arriving late at a dance.

Anne and Michelle strolled by Eileen's side. It was their last time together before she left for Ireland, and they'd booked a table in the beer garden of the Bowling Green for goodbye drinks later. Michelle had insisted on sitting outside, even though restrictions on the two-metre rule had been lifted and they'd all had their second jabs. Slithers of honey-coloured evening sunlight dropped onto the path in front of them as they walked. It had been a few weeks since they'd seen each other. They'd all been busy getting back to the new normal, whatever that was. Eileen had been tying up loose ends at college and sorting out the move, Anne had returned to Clay Corner, and Michelle, despite going part-time at the hospital, was inundated with a backlog of non-Covid admissions.

Eileen inhaled the earthy smell left by the earlier rain. "I'm going to miss the Meadows," she said.

"It won't be the same without you," Michelle replied quietly.

"I googled the Wild Atlantic Way last night," said Anne. "I'm still not sure what it is, but I can't wait to visit."

Eileen smiled. She'd always thought the landscape at home was very different to the English landscape. Here there was a tranquillity in the rolling hills, valleys, and woodlands. By contrast, the rugged mountains and savage coastline of the west of Ireland were unsettling. It didn't calm, it made her heart leap and her spirits roar and she longed to be enveloped in it again. Windy Sunday walks in Connemara with the rain lashing her face, warm days on Keem Bay beach in Achill, ferry trips to Clare Island. She couldn't wait. She might even climb the Reek again with Shannon like they did when they were teenagers.

Michelle started to hum the tune of "Take me Home to Mayo", a popular Irish ballad. She glanced at Eileen. "Did you know that song's about an IRA hunger striker who died in jail here?"

"I did, actually."

Wincing at the mention of the IRA, Eileen looked over at Anne who was trailing her eyes on the ground. She thought about the extraordinary story she had told her about her father, how she thought he'd been killed by an IRA bomb planted under his car, but had recently discovered that he'd got into the car knowing it was there. She'd been devastated to find out he'd committed suicide. And, to top it all, Michelle's Uncle Jimmy had emerged as a possible suspect in the planting of the bomb. How mad was that?

In all the years they'd known each other, Anne had rarely spoken about her father to them. She told them he was a colonel in the British army, and that he'd died young, but that was about it. She never once hinted at any IRA involvement in his death, probably because of Michelle's republican family. Looking back there were clues, though. Moments when Anne would let her guard down. Like the time she'd stormed off outside Waxy O'Connor's, when she and Michelle were singing rebel songs, or the way she'd always get prickly and change the subject if Irish politics came up. Once, Michelle had asked her if she thought Anne was anti-Irish.

"I wouldn't say anti-Irish," she had replied. "But she's definitely wary of us at times."

Poor lovely Anne. Locking up all that sadness inside her for years. When Eileen asked her if she was ever going to tell Michelle about her Uncle Jimmy being a suspect, she'd said, "What's the point? Michelle's been through enough as it is. She doesn't need to know that about her uncle. Anyway, I have no proof he was involved, and he's dead, so I'll never know." After she'd said it, she had given Eileen a lingering, probing look. "It's not always best to tell people the brutal truth about their loved ones. Some things are better left unsaid."

Then she had looked away, flustered, as if she'd spoken out of place. At that moment, Eileen knew that the brutal truth she was referring to was Carla and Sergio's affair.

She'd made the decision not to talk about the affair to anyone, not even Michelle. But she had asked herself many times if Anne knew. She wasn't that surprised to find out that apparently she did, but she was hurt. They had been friends for so long. Why hadn't Anne told her? Where was her loyalty? As a result, Eileen avoided her for months. Eventually she came to her senses. She was about to leave for Ireland. What was the point of destroying a twenty-year friendship over it? Life was too short. Besides, who knows what she'd have done in Anne's shoes?

It was nine long months since she had found Carla's email on Sergio's laptop. When she confronted him, he admitted everything straightaway. He said it was the biggest mistake of his life and he followed her around for days, pleading for forgiveness.

"I was depressed and in a dark place," he said, reaching for her. "It was a moment of excitement."

She pushed him away, no longer tempted by his touch. "How do I know it's over?"

"When you saw the email, did you find a reply from me? No. Because I stopped all contact. It's over. She means nothing to me. It was sex, nothing more."

He moved into the box-room. For months, tension crackled in the air and the long silences between them were interspersed with fierce arguments. When Alex asked what was going on, she told him the truth. Was it any wonder he escaped to Dublin the first chance he got?

For weeks she tossed and turned in bed at night, listening to Sergio moving around in the box-room. She remembered the dream she used to have about the renovated farmhouse in Mayo. In it, Alex was always smiling, but Sergio never was. Was the dream telling her something she didn't want to admit? That deep down, she'd always known Sergio was never committed to the move to Ireland?

"I swear, I want to go," he insisted when she probed him, "It will be a new start for us."

"I'm going whether you're coming or not," she replied.

And she meant every word.

Two months after the second lockdown ended, they finally sold the Chorlton house to a young couple from Blackpool with a new-born. The Mayo house was more or less built and the removal van was coming on Monday. Her teaching job in the community college started mid-September, so they had the whole summer to settle in. Eileen still pinched herself now and again. Was she really going home after all these years?

A group of cyclists whizzed past, forcing the three women off the path and into the bushes.

"Lycra lunatics!" yelled Anne, giving them the finger and brushing herself down. She turned to Eileen. "What's Alex's news? Is he still enjoying Dublin?"

"Loving it, apart from the flat-hunting. There's hardly anything available to rent. They're still staying with Ross's parents in Howth, but it's a huge house, so it's not really a problem. Alex is working in a restaurant nearby."

Anne placed her right hand on her heart. "Such a happy ending to a pandemic romance."

Eileen smiled. "I don't think Ross returned from New York just to be with Alex. He was planning to come back anyway after Covid. That said, it does seem pretty serious between them."

"And does Alex still want to train to be a paramedic?" asked Michelle.

Eileen nodded. "The plan is to continue with the bar work until he gets his residency, then he'll apply."

Anne's phone rang. When she stopped to answer it, Eileen and Michelle stood and waited. Eileen spotted a Red Admiral butterfly on a gorse bush beside them. It was tiny and could only just have transitioned from being a caterpillar. She beckoned to Michelle, and they both watched in awe as it fluttered its miniscule black-and-orange wings and tentatively took flight.

When Anne had finished her call, she slipped her phone into her bag and hurried towards them. "Sorry about that. Meg's having issues with the oven at Clay Corner. I don't think I've told you her latest. She says the past year at uni has been a write-off, so she's decided to transfer to psychology in September. Apparently, she wants to work in mental health."

"Really?" Michelle's face brightened.

Anne laughed. "Can you believe it? All those times I had to drag her kicking and screaming to see a therapist, and now she wants to be one." She shrugged. "She still has her own ups and downs, but we'll support her, if that's what she wants to do. Hakim's happy about it because he thinks there's a good chance of a job at the end of it."

"He's right," said Michelle. "They're crying out for mental-health workers post Covid. And Meg will make a smashing therapist. I don't know what Nathan would have done without her this past year."

Anne linked arms with Michelle. "They're such good buddies, aren't they? Meg tells me he's got a job at the pizza place on Beech Road."

Michelle nodded. "Small steps, and all that."

Anne and Eileen waited for her to say more, but she didn't. These days she rarely volunteered much information about Nathan at all.

Eileen had been shocked to the core the night Anne rang to tell her that Nathan had attempted suicide. It was the night she discovered Sergio's infidelity, and she was in an awful state, but when Anne suggested they go to the hospital to be with Michelle, she couldn't refuse. Michelle was on her own and her best friend. How could she leave her in her darkest hour?

It was a cold evening and visitors weren't allowed inside the hospital. She and Anne shivered on the bench outside the A&E department, waiting for Michelle to come out to them.

"I can't believe it," said Eileen, shaking her head, "He was so sure of himself. So confident. Nothing seemed to touch him."

"They're the ones to watch for," replied Anne. "The quiet ones who wear the mask well, the ones who bottle everything up, the ones afraid to show weakness, or admit there's anything wrong. They're often men. My father was like that. I'm pretty sure if he'd got help for his mental health, he'd be alive today."

The next morning Eileen woke Alex and told him the news. He sat up bolt right in bed and rubbed his eyes.

"No way. Nathan? You're kidding me," he said.

She sat at the edge of his bed.

He stared down at his duvet. She waited for him to process it.

He looked up at last.

"Some students at the uni were posting stuff about him on social media," he said.

"Michelle mentioned something about that last night. What kind of stuff?"

"They were calling him out for some videos he'd posted. Stupid, sexist and racist stuff. Knowing Nathan, he probably thought they were edgy and funny."

"When was this?"

"A few months ago. Meg told me all his mates dropped him."

"You mean he was cancelled? That's what you call it, isn't it?"

"I suppose so."

Eileen shook her head. "And the poor boy not long after losing his father. To be hung, drawn and quartered on social media and lose all his friends for a couple of stupid videos? Come on. The punishment hardly fits the crime."

Alex leaned back against the pillows. "The people who did it would say they were holding him to account for the things he'd posted. We've known him for years, Mum. We both know he probably did say and do some of those things."

Eileen sighed. "I know, but still …"

"Did you know he got thrown off his course?"

Alex nodded. "Meg told me."

They both fell into a thoughtful silence.

"You two grew up together," she said, running a finger along the duvet. "There was a time, when you were fifteen or sixteen, when you'd have done anything for Nathan."

"I know." Alex reddened. "I had a massive crush on him for ages." He swallowed and looked like he was about to cry. "Jesus, Mum. I can't believe he tried to take his own life."

A gentle breeze wafted in the trees as they crossed the iron bridge by the brook.

Anne turned to Michelle. "Seen Amir recently?" she asked with a sly smile.

Michelle, head bent deep in thought, looked up and blushed. "Get lost. We're old friends."

Anne grinned. "People don't snog old friends, darling."

Michelle looked back down at the ground and smiled. "We're taking it slowly."

"He's so into you, Michelle," said Eileen. "And he's a dote. Definitely a keeper."

The one thing Eileen didn't want to leave behind in Manchester was Michelle. If she could, she'd wrap her up and place her in the back of the removal van with the sofas and chairs and install her in the new house in Mayo. Knowing that she was in a relationship with Amir made leaving all that bit easier. Michelle hadn't been the same person since Nathan's suicide attempt. She had been through so much already: the split with Billy, Rob's death, and the hell of working at the hospital through Covid. What happened with Nathan had almost broken her. For months afterwards, she seemed to operate in a daze, the weight of her trauma dragging her down like a heavy cloak, slowing the spring in her step and crushing her feisty spirit.

When he was first discharged from hospital, Nathan told Michelle he'd taken the overdose in a moment of madness. He swore he was fine and refused counselling. Unconvinced, Michelle watched him like a hawk. During the second lockdown, he fell into another deep depression, telling Michelle he wanted to harm himself again. This time, with Meg's help, he finally agreed to go to grief-counselling and try anti-depressants. Michelle had told her recently she was now noticing small improvements in his mood.

Eileen had bumped into him outside the Co-op on Beech Road at Christmas. He'd put on a lot of weight and his handsome, chiselled face was now hidden behind an unkempt bushy beard and folds of fat. She tried to engage him in conversation, but he'd given her a gruff nod and walked away. As she watched him go, she was overcome with sadness as she remembered the cheeky, boisterous young boy she'd known since birth.

A sharp chill nipping at her bare arms, Eileen slipped on the Aran jumper she'd been wearing around her waist. As she pulled it over her head, she could hear faint music coming from the field on the other side of a hawthorn bush nearby.

"I can smell weed, can you?" said Anne.

The three of them peeped through the yellow flowers into the field where a group of teens were sitting around in a circle. They looked about fifteen or sixteen. Some were goths, others grungy-looking, and some picked nervously at clumps of grass. Empty bottles and cans were scattered at their feet, and a couple of speakers stood in the middle of the circle. One of the boys, slim with long dark hair flopping down over his eyes, reminded Eileen of Alex at that age. She thought about him and Meg and Nathan. The past few years had been tumultuous for their entire generation. The global upheaval and drastic changes in society had completely derailed their path to adulthood. God love them. Surely the worst was now behind them?

Suddenly, a couple of the girls in the group stood up. Laughing, they pulled their friends to their feet. One of them went over to one of the speakers and turned up the volume. Then, under a sunset of fiery reds and oranges, they slowly raised their arms and, one by one, they started to dance.

THE END

Printed in Great Britain
by Amazon